Exploring Music History

A Guided Approach

Volume 1

Baroque to the Modern Era

by
Janet Lopinski, Joe Ringhofer,
and Peteris Zarins

National Library of Canada Cataloguing in Publication Data

Lopinski, Janet Marie
Exploring music history : a guided approach / Janet Lopinski, Joe Ringhofer, Peteris Zarins.

Contents: v. 1. Baroque to the modern era – v. 2. Middle ages to classical – v. 3. 19th and 20th centuries.
ISBN 0-88797-824-X (v. 1). – ISBN 0-88797-826-6 (v. 2). – ISBN 0-88797-783-9 (v. 3).

1. Music – History and criticism – Instruction and study – Activity programs.
2. Music – History and criticism – Problems, exercises, etc.
I. Ringhofer, Joe J. II. Zarins, Peteris III. Title.

ML193.L748 2002 780'.9 C2002-900878-6

ISBN 978-0-88797-824-1

FREDERICK HARRIS MUSIC

Contents

UNIT THREE – The Classical Period 51

UNIT FOUR – The Romantic Period 94

APPENDICES

Preface

This book is the first of a three-volume series entitled *Exploring Music History: A Guided Approach.* These three workbooks are intended to support students and teachers preparing for The Royal Conservatory of Music (RCM) history examinations as outlined in the *Theory Syllabus,* 2002 edition. They will also be useful to students whose goal is simply to explore music history for the sake of becoming better informed as musicians and listeners.

Volume 1 serves as an introduction to the study of music history and is intended to prepare students for the RCM History 1: An Overview (Grade 3 History) Examination. Representative composers and works from four of the major periods in music history—Baroque, Classical, Romantic, and 20th century—are presented. Emphasis is placed on developing familiarity with the lives and musical styles of selected composers and exploring a wide variety of musical genres and forms.

This is not a textbook. We assume that students will be working with an introductory music history or music appreciation textbook, using music dictionaries or encyclopedias, doing internet research, and/or attending lectures or classes given by a qualified teacher. We also expect that students will listen to recordings of the works studied—not doing so would be like studying art history without viewing a single painting! Whenever possible, it would be beneficial for students to examine musical scores while completing listening activities. For a list of recommended resources that includes books, encyclopedias, websites, videos, and DVDs, please consult Appendix A. Appendix B lists recommended listening materials for all required pieces in this volume. In Appendix C, we have provided a template for a listening report that can be assigned as homework.

This volume contains a variety of activities that require both writing and listening. Terms necessary to understand and describe music are introduced in segments entitled "Building a Musical Vocabulary." For each major composer, the heading "The Life and Music of..." is used. Specific compositions to be studied are identified by the heading "Required Listening." Other listening activities involve the identification of musical or stylistic elements in familiar works from the era being examined. At the end of each unit a section entitled "Review and Reflection" helps students synthesize the information presented and invites personal opinions. Each unit concludes with a short quiz.

Since we believe that the study of music history can and should be both interesting and enjoyable, we have included additional items and activities to enrich the learning experience and give students a broader perspective. The heading "Did You Know?" is used to present interesting or unusual facts and stories. Computer-savvy students are invited to use the internet in a series of "Web Quests." The heading "Supplemental Activity" is used for additional tasks such as completing maps and diagrams, looking at artwork, and watching films. We have also made recommendations for additional listening throughout the book; these lists appear at the end of each section devoted to an individual composer.

We hope that upon completing this book, students will have developed a familiarity with the musical styles of the Baroque, Classical, Romantic, and 20th-century periods, and as a result, perform music—and listen to it—with deeper understanding.

Janet Lopinski, Joe Ringhofer, Peteris Zarins

Acknowledgements

The authors would like to thank the following people for their valuable assistance in preparing this publication:

Dr. Laura Beauchamp, Editor
Dr. Trish Sauerbrei, Editor-in-Chief, The Frederick Harris Music Co., Limited
Jennifer de Boer, Project Administrator

Grateful acknowledgement is due to the following publisher for permission granted to use excerpts from the music listed below:

UNIT ONE

THE MATERIALS OF MUSIC

Every successful journey requires careful preparation. As we embark on our exploration of music history, it is important to establish basic terminology and acquire a common vocabulary with which we can discuss music and write about it intelligently.

Building A Musical Vocabulary: *Elements of Music*

Melody

What often attracts us to a musical composition and later lingers in our memories is the melody. While adjectives such as "beautiful," "flowing," and "elegant" may reflect the listener's reactions, they do little to communicate the nature of a melody. The terms that follow are used by musicians to describe melodic characteristics.

Match each term to the appropriate definition below:

conjunct	interval	phrase	range
disjunct	motive	pitch	

________________ The highness or lowness of a particular sound.

________________ The distance between the highest and lowest notes of a melody.

________________ The distance between any two pitches.

________________ Melodies that move mostly in a stepwise direction.

________________ Melodies containing many leaps and changes of direction.

________________ A series of consecutive pitches forming a musical unit much like a sentence.

________________ A short melodic or rhythmic fragment used in the building of a melody.

Rhythm

Just as the heartbeat creates a natural pulse in our bodies to maintain a life force, rhythm animates a musical composition. The following terms are fundamental in describing the rhythmic aspects of music.

Match each term to the appropriate definition below:

anacrusis	measure	simple time
compound time	meter	syncopation
hemiola	ostinato	

_______________ A metrical unit containing a fixed number of beats separated on the musical staff by bar lines.

_______________ Fixed patterns of strong and weak beats.

_______________ Time signatures in which each beat contains two subdivisions.

_______________ Time signatures in which each beat contains three (rather than two) subdivisions.

_______________ A deliberate shifting of the musical accent to a weak beat.

_______________ An upbeat, or the last beat of a measure anticipating the downbeat.

_______________ A short rhythmic or melodic pattern repeated for an extended period.

_______________ A temporary shift of the metric accents created by using two notes in the time of three, or three notes in the time of two.

Harmony

Another dimension is added to music through harmony, which supports the melody and provides context. Melody and harmony are interdependent.

Match each term to the appropriate definition below:

cadence	consonance	harmonic rhythm
chord	diatonic	triad
chromatic	dissonance	

_______________ A combination of three or more pitches creating a unit of harmony.

_______________ A three-note chord consisting of a root, third, and fifth.

_______________ Melodies/harmonies built from the notes of a major or minor scale.

_______________ Melodies/harmonies including all the notes available within the octave; from the Greek word for "color."

_______________ An agreeable combination of tones that provides a sense of relaxation and stability.

_______________ A combination of tones that sounds discordant, thus creating restlessness and a sense of instability.

______________ The rate (frequency) of chord changes per measure.

______________ A specific combination of two chords providing moments of rest at the ends of phrases, much like punctuation.

Texture

Just as our clothing is woven from different fabrics, music can have various textures. Match each term to the appropriate definition below:

monophonic polyphonic homophonic

______________ A single line of unaccompanied melody.

______________ A single line of melody supported by a harmonic accompaniment.

______________ A combination of two or more melodic lines. Also referred to as *counterpoint*.

Additional Terms

The terms listed below will also prove useful in your descriptions of musical compositions. Provide a definition for each:

dynamics ______________

timbre ______________

tempo ______________

genre ______________

opus ______________

idiomatic writing ______________

Listening For Musical Elements

Listen to a recording or performance of *Invention in F Major,* BWV 779 by J.S. Bach and *Für Elise,* WoO 59 by Ludwig van Beethoven. Study the excerpts below, then answer the questions.

Ex. 1.1 Bach, *Invention in F Major*, BWV 779.

Ex. 1.2 Beethoven, *Für Elise*, WoO 59.

	Bach, *Invention in F Major*	Beethoven, *Für Elise*
The melody is more:	☐ conjunct ☐ disjunct	☐ conjunct ☐ disjunct
The meter is:	☐ simple time ☐ compound time	☐ simple time ☐ compound time
The texture is:	☐ homophonic ☐ polyphonic	☐ homophonic ☐ polyphonic
The melody is:	☐ strictly diatonic ☐ chromatic	☐ strictly diatonic ☐ chromatic
The piece begins:	☐ with an anacrusis ☐ on the downbeat	☐ with an anacrusis ☐ on the downbeat
The range of the melody is:	☐ within the 8^{ve} ☐ beyond the 8^{ve}	☐ within the 8^{ve} ☐ beyond the 8^{ve}

Performing Forces

A musical composition is brought to life through performance. Each voice, or instrument, can be identified by its own unique tone quality or color.

Voice Types

The oldest and most natural instrument is the human voice. Voice types are designated according to their range.

Identify the four principal voice types:

High female voice ____________________

Low female voice ____________________

High male voice ____________________

Low male voice ____________________

Define the following additional voice classifications:

baritone ____________________

mezzo-soprano ____________________

coloratura soprano ____________________

Keyboard Instruments

Briefly describe the following keyboard instruments. How is the sound produced on each?

organ ____________________

piano ____________________

harpsichord ____________________

clavichord ____________________

accordion ____

____

____

synthesizer ____

____

____

Orchestral Instruments

The orchestra is a large ensemble consisting of many contrasting instruments. The instruments of the orchestra are classified into four families or groups: *string, woodwind, brass,* and *percussion.* In the chart below, classify each orchestral instrument by putting a check under its appropriate group.

INSTRUMENT	STRING	WOODWIND	BRASS	PERCUSSION
contrabassoon				
flute				
cymbals				
violin				
glockenspiel				
French horn				
English horn				
timpani				
bass clarinet				
piccolo				
trumpet				
viola				
snare drum				
oboe				
celesta				
violoncello				
clarinet				
tuba				
xylophone				
tambourine				
saxophone				
double bass				
triangle				
bassoon				
castanets				
trombone				

Within each family of instruments, there is diversity and variety not only in size but also in construction. Fill in the blanks below, identifying the instruments described:

single reed woodwind instruments ______________ ______________

double reed woodwind instruments ______________ ______________

pitched percussion instruments ______________ ______________

non-pitched percussion instruments ______________ ______________

lowest sounding instrument in the brass family ______________

highest sounding instrument in the woodwind family ______________

brass instrument with a slide ______________

plucked string instrument with pedals ______________

Chamber Music Ensembles

Music written for small ensembles with one player per part is referred to as *chamber music*. This term reflects the intimate settings in which the music was first performed. Historically, chamber music was presented in the salons of patrons who had sponsored the works.

Listed below are four standard chamber music ensembles. Identify the instruments included in each:

1. String Quartet ______________ ______________

   ______________ ______________

2. Piano Trio ______________ ______________

   ____

3. Woodwind Quintet ______________ ______________

   ______________ ______________

   ____

4. Brass Quintet ______________ ______________

   ______________ ______________

   ____

Although the instruments of each family are generally grouped together, the actual arrangement of those families on the concert stage may vary from orchestra to orchestra.

WEB QUEST

Would you recognize the major instruments if you heard them? Do you know what they look like and where they are located in the orchestra? Use your search engine to find pictures and sound clips of instruments and diagrams of orchestra layouts. Try key words and phrases like *symphony, orchestra, instrument families, orchestra layout.*

Supplemental Activity: *Seating Plan of an Orchestra*

In the space provided, draw the seating plan of a standard symphony orchestra.

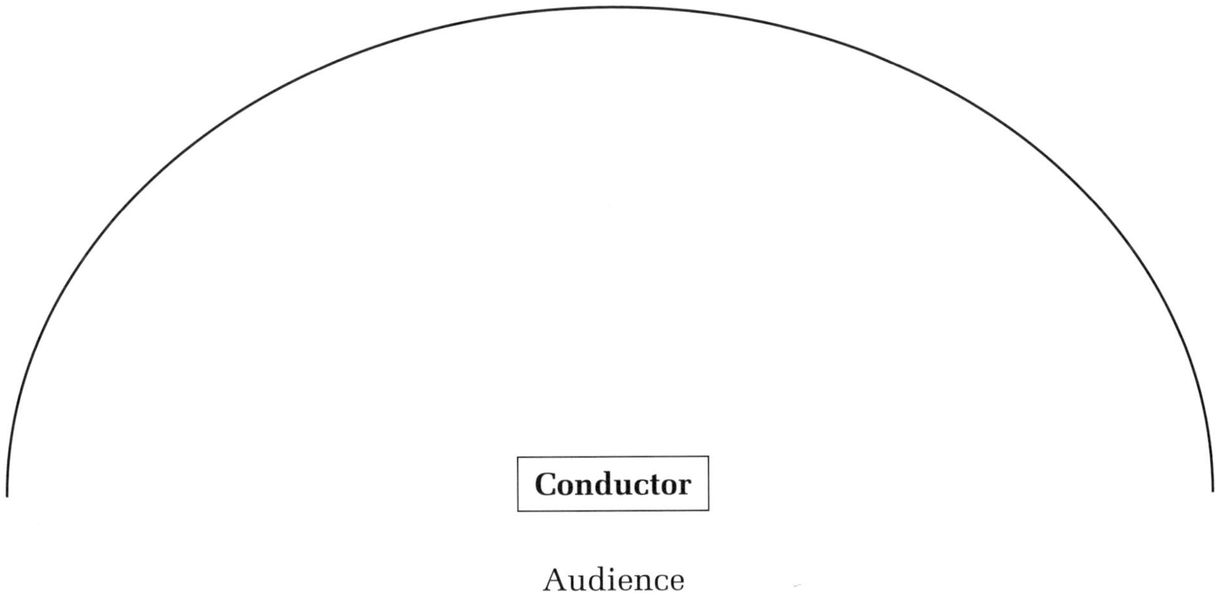

Required Listening: *The Young Person's Guide to the Orchestra*

In 1946, the noted English composer Benjamin Britten (1913–1976) was commissioned by the British Broadcasting Corporation (BBC) to create a large-scale orchestral work that would introduce young audiences to the instruments of the orchestra. This work is an excellent point of departure for our study of music history because it will help us to become familiar with orchestral instruments.

Listen to a recording of *The Young Person's Guide to the Orchestra* and answer the following questions:

Subtitle ______________________________

Britten based this work on a dance tune by Henry Purcell. Who was he?

____

____

Part 1: Theme

Ex. 1.3 Britten, *The Young Person's Guide to the Orchestra*/I, mm. 1-8.

In this opening section, the melody shown in Ex. 1.3 is projected clearly, supported by harmonic accompaniment. Circle the term below which describes the texture in this section:

monophonic texture　　　polyphonic texture　　　homophonic texture

The principal theme is stated six times, with full orchestra featured in the first and sixth statements. Name the orchestral family featured in each of the remaining sections:

1. *full orchestra*
2. ________________
3. ________________
4. ________________
5. ________________
6. *full orchestra*

Part 2: Variations

Part 2 consists of thirteen short variations, each introducing a different instrument. Identify the solo instrument(s) featured in each variation, and its family.

1. ________________　________________
2. ________________　________________
3. ________________　________________
4. ________________　________________
5. ________________　________________
6. ________________　________________

7. ____________________ ____________________

8. ____________________ ____________________

9. ____________________ ____________________

10. ____________________ ____________________

11. ____________________ ____________________

12. ____________________ ____________________

13. various percussion instruments—identify four

____________ ____________ ____________ ____________

Part 3: Fugue

Ex. 1.4 Britten, *The Young Person's Guide to the Orchestra*/III, fugue theme.

The *fugue* was a form favored by composers in the Baroque era, most notably J.S. Bach. Provide a brief definition of fugue.

____

____

____

In fugal analysis, what is the opening theme called?

____

Compare the order in which the instruments enter in this fugue to the order in which they appear in the thirteen variations.

____

____

Which musical themes does Britten bring together to form the climax and conclusion of this work?

____________________ and ____________________

Timeline:
Four Major Style Periods in Music History

As a prelude to our exploration of music and composers from the Baroque, Classical, Romantic, and 20th-century periods, it is important to cast an eye over the "big picture" to place our detailed study into a broader context. The timeline below shows the composers you will study in this workbook. Add the titles of compositions you have played recently, placing them in the appropriate era.

1600–1750	1750–1825	1825–1900	1900–2000
Baroque	**Classical**	**Romantic**	**20th Century** (Modern Era)
Antonio Vivaldi Johann Sebastian Bach George Frideric Handel	Franz Joseph Haydn Wolfgang Amadeus Mozart Ludwig van Beethoven	Franz Schubert Frédéric Chopin Hector Berlioz Georges Bizet Giacomo Puccini	Claude Debussy Igor Stravinsky Leonard Bernstein Alexina Louie
My Repertoire __________ __________	__________ __________	__________ __________	__________ __________

WEB QUEST

Would you recognize the major composers from the Baroque, Classical, Romantic, and 20th-century periods if you saw their portraits? Use your search engine to find paintings or photographs of the musicians listed in the timeline. Compile your own music history portrait gallery.

Review and Reflection

Name five prominent performers of your principal instrument. Who is your personal favorite? You may enjoy learning more about these artists by searching the internet for information about them.

________________ ________________ ________________

________________ ________________

What other instruments do you or members of your family play?

____

Quiz

Identify each instrument shown and the orchestral family to which it belongs:

1

2
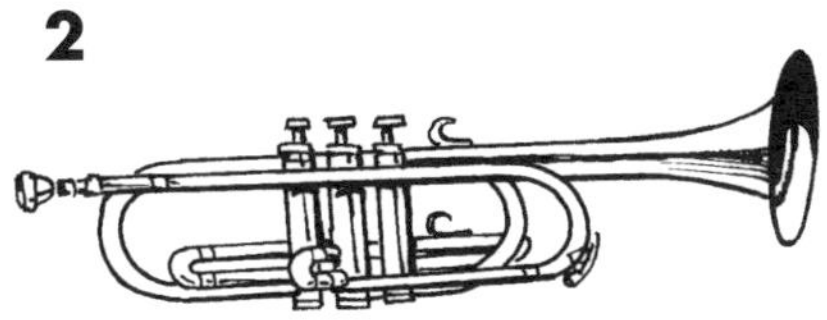

11
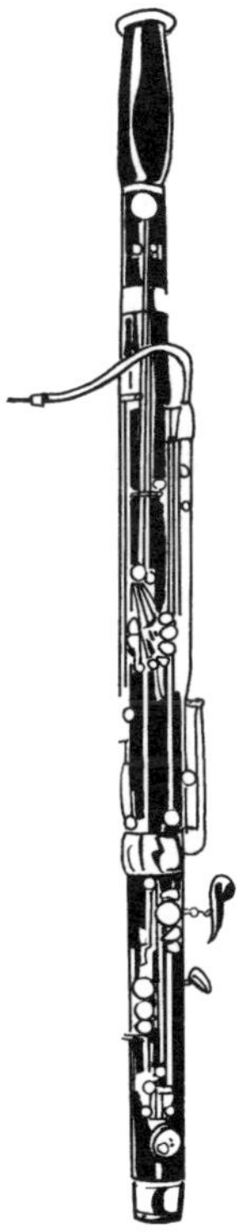

1. snare drum ______ percussion ______
2. ______ ______
3. ______ ______
4. ______ ______
5. ______ ______
6. ______ ______
7. ______ ______
8. ______ ______
9. ______ ______
10. ______ ______
11. ______ ______

3

4

10
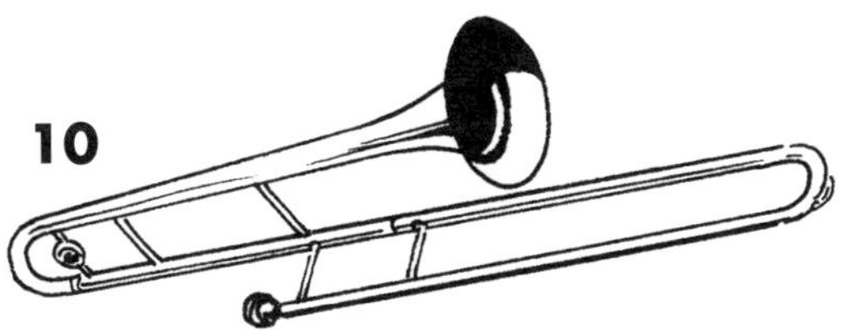

5

9
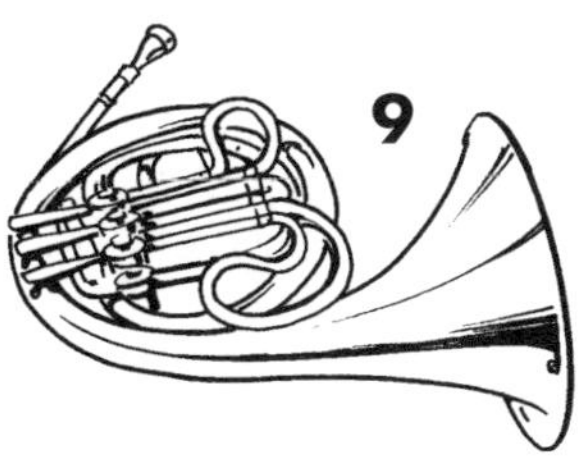

7
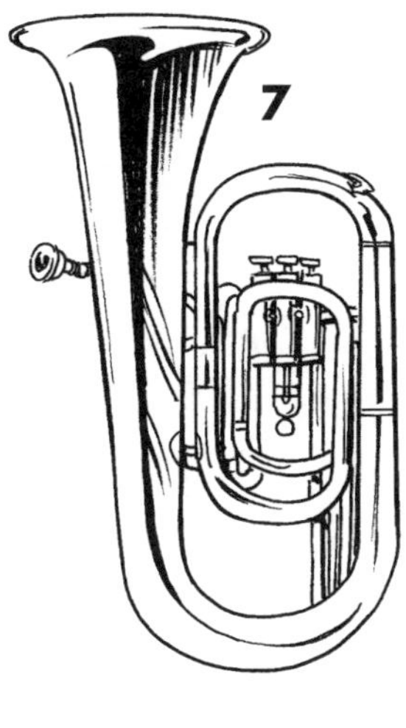

6
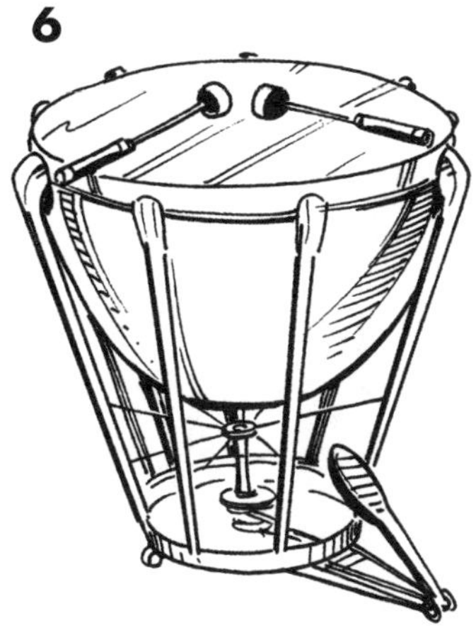

8
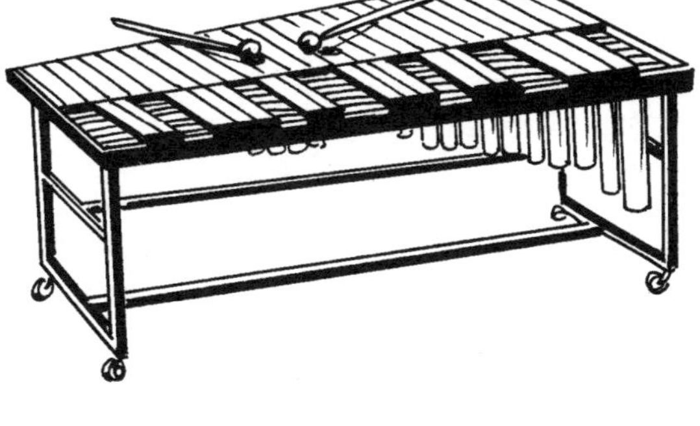

UNIT TWO

THE BAROQUE PERIOD (1600–1750)

The Baroque period was a time of turbulence, contrasts, and change. These qualities are reflected in the art and music of the period. In the study of music history, the dates chosen to define the Baroque era represent major milestones: 1600 coincides with the birth of opera, while 1750 marks the death of J.S. Bach. In between, many new forms, genres, and textures emerged, and new instruments were developed. The crystallization of the major-minor system provided the harmonic backbone of Baroque style. Additionally, instrumental music began to stand shoulder to shoulder with vocal music.

Before we embark on our exploration of Baroque music, you should have an overview of the cultural and historical events of the time. Examine the timeline below to see how many people and events you recognize. In the space provided, add four additional events or people of interest to you.

Timeline

1600 – 1750

Historical Events	• **1607** First European settlement in America founded at Jamestown, Virginia; • **1615** Galileo faces Inquisition; • **1637** First public opera house opens in Venice; • **1643** Reign of Louis XIV begins; • ***ca* 1700** Piano invented; • **1726** Gulliver's Travels published; • **1749** Fort established at Toronto, Canada
Important Figures	**René Descartes** 1596–1650; **Rembrandt van Rijn** 1606–1684; **Antonio Stradiveri** 1644–1737; **Francois Voltaire** 1694–1778
Composers	**Claudio Monteverdi** 1567–1643; **J.B. Lully** 1632–1687; **Arcangelo Corelli** 1653–1713; **Henry Purcell** 1659–1695; **Antonio Vivaldi** 1678–1741; **G.P. Telemann** 1681–1767; **Domenico Scarlatti** 1685–1757; **Johann Sebastian Bach** 1685–1750; **George Frideric Handel** 1685–1759
Additional Events/People	

Historical and Cultural Background

Explain the origins of the term *Baroque*.

List four characteristics of Baroque art and architecture:

1. ornate
2.
3.
4.

Throughout the Baroque period, there were continuous advancements and discoveries in the arts and sciences. Comment briefly on the significance of the leading cultural figures listed below:

Isaac Newton — English scientist and mathematician. Discovered the principle of gravity, developed calculus. Explored the science of the color spectrum.

Galileo Galilei

John Milton

Rembrandt

J.B. Molière

UNIT TWO

William Harvey ______________________________

____

____

Peter Paul Rubens ______________________________

____

____

WEB QUEST

Use the internet to learn more about the important cultural figures and developments from the Baroque era. For example, find paintings by Rembrandt and Rubens, or locate some of the ornate buildings (like the palace at Versailles) that exemplify Baroque architectural style.

Building a Musical Vocabulary: *Elements of Baroque Style*

As we begin our study of specific composers and works from the Baroque era, we will discover certain recurring characteristics and common features. Define the terms below as they apply to Baroque musical style:

figured bass ______________________________

____

____

basso continuo ______________________________

____

____

major-minor tonality ______________________________

____

____

counterpoint ______________________________

____

____

monody ______________________________

____

____

improvisation ______________________________

____

____

binary form ______________________________

____

____

ternary form ______________________________

____

____

Match the following terms with the definitions given below:

The Affections	Florentine Camerata
Collegium musicum	*Le nuove musiche*
Equal temperament	Word painting

______________ A group of Italian artists, writers, and musicians who sought to revive Greek drama, leading to the birth of opera.

______________ An expressive device in which the meaning of the words is vividly depicted through the music.

______________ A philosophy which sought to project one clear emotion for the duration of a composition or movement.

______________ "The New Music" (1602) by Giulio Caccini, containing solo songs using a new musical style called *monody*.

______________ Association of amateur musicians often based in university settings.

______________ A new system of tuning keyboard instruments in which all semitones (half-steps) are equal.

Comment briefly on each of the following as they relate to Baroque music:

dance types ______________________________

____

____

____

idiomatic writing

dynamics

rhythm

ornamentation

virtuosity

patronage of the arts

Listening for Elements of Baroque Style

Part One:

Listen to one of the following works by J.S. Bach. If possible, follow a score while you listen.

Concerto for Two Violins in D Minor, BWV 1043 (First Movement)
Brandenburg Concerto No. 4, BWV 1049 (First Movement)

From the list below, identify the Baroque style features you hear in the performance. If you have a score, which additional features do you notice?

- ☐ figured bass
- ☐ basso continuo
- ☐ major-minor tonality
- ☐ counterpoint
- ☐ idiomatic writing
- ☐ improvisation
- ☐ dance rhythms
- ☐ virtuosity
- ☐ ornamentation
- ☐ terraced dynamics
- ☐ motoric rhythm

Part Two:
Identify one Baroque work in your own repertoire. Which features from the above list apply to your piece?

Title ____

Composer ____

Instrument ____

Musical features ____

____

____

____

____

Vivaldi and *The Four Seasons*

Some pieces of music are instantly recognizable. Such is the case with *The Four Seasons*. Among the thousands of concertos written in the Baroque period, and the hundreds written by Vivaldi himself, this work has earned a special place in the repertoire. It is one of the most widely recorded Baroque musical compositions.

The Life and Music of Antonio Vivaldi (1678–1741)

In his musical career, Vivaldi was a violinist, conductor, and highly prolific composer of many genres. Although he regarded himself primarily as a composer of opera, his fame today rests largely on his contributions to the Baroque concerto repertoire. Vivaldi's brilliant, idiomatic writing for strings advanced the art of performance to new heights of virtuosity.

What was Vivaldi's nationality? ____________________

What was his father's profession? ____________________

With which city did he maintain a life-long association? ____________________

Vivaldi served as *maestro di' concerti* (music director) at a music school for orphan girls for many years. What was the name of the school?

____

What was Vivaldi's other vocation? ____________________

In what city did Vivaldi spend his final days? ____________________

What contributions did Vivaldi make to the development of violin technique and style?

____

____

____

____

____

Check the boxes that accurately complete the following statements about Vivaldi's musical style:

Vivaldi's concertos most often employ:
- ☐ three-movement form
- ☐ four-movement form
- ☐ five-movement form

Vivaldi composed:
- ☐ only one opera
- ☐ over ten operas
- ☐ over forty operas

L'Estro armonico is:
- ☐ an opera by Vivaldi
- ☐ an oratorio by Vivaldi
- ☐ a set of concertos by Vivaldi

Vivaldi contributed to the development of:
- ☐ ritornello form
- ☐ sonata-allegro form
- ☐ binary form

Many of Vivaldi's compositions were published in:
- ☐ Amsterdam
- ☐ London
- ☐ New York

One composer who transcribed several of Vivaldi's concertos was:
- ☐ Caccini
- ☐ J.S. Bach
- ☐ Haydn

Juditha Triumphans is:
- ☐ an opera by Vivaldi
- ☐ an oratorio by Vivaldi
- ☐ a concerto by Vivaldi

Composers who influenced the development of Vivaldi's compositional style include:

- ☐ Lully and Rameau
- ☐ Corelli and Torelli
- ☐ Léonin and Pérotin

Several of Vivaldi's instrumental works display:

- ☐ descriptive (programmatic) elements
- ☐ modal writing
- ☐ chorale variations

Vivaldi was known as:

- ☐ the "red priest"
- ☐ the "poet of the piano"
- ☐ the "father of the string quartet"

Building a Musical Vocabulary: *The Baroque Concerto*

Explain the origin of the term *concerto.*

____

____

____

____

Identify and describe the two types of concertos written in the Baroque era.

1. ________________

____

____

____

2. ________________

____

____

____

Explain the following components as they relate to the Baroque concerto:

ritornello form ________________________________

____

____

____

UNIT TWO

tutti/ripieno ______________________________

____

____

____

concertino ______________________________

____

____

____

Required Listening: *Spring* from *The Four Seasons*, op. 8, no. 1

Listen to a recording of *Spring* from *The Four Seasons*. If possible, follow a score while you listen. Answer the questions below:

The Four Seasons comprises the first four of a set of twelve concertos published as Vivaldi's op. 8. This collection was subtitled "Il cimento dell'armonia e dell'invenzione."

Translate the subtitle into English. ______________________________

What do you suppose Vivaldi was suggesting with this description?

____

____

____

What are the original Italian titles of *The Four Seasons* and *Spring?*

____

What type of concerto is *Spring*? ______________________________

Vivaldi used a poem as the basis for this composition. What type of poem was it, and who was the likely author? ______________________________

What type of spring-like images does this poem depict?

____

____

____

What is the instrumentation of the first and third movements?

Ripieno ______________________ Soloist ______________________

____

____

____

____

In the second movement, the instrumentation is reduced. Which instruments remain?

______________________ ______________________

______________________ ______________________

In *The Four Seasons*, Vivaldi utilizes *word painting*, a technique usually associated with vocal music but applied here in an instrumental context. What is word painting in music?

____

____

____

How did Vivaldi indicate which poetic images he was representing musically?

____

____

____

Listed below are several poetic images from *Spring*. For each of the musical excerpts that follow, identify which poetic image is being represented and what musical elements are used to create the image. (The first example has been completed to guide you.)

Poetic images:

- Nymphs and shepherds dancing in the fields to the happy sounds of bagpipes
- Thunder and lightning
- The joyful arrival of spring
- A sleeping goatherd with his faithful dog barking at his side
- The joyful song of the birds
- The sweet murmur of the gentle breezes

Ex. 2.1 Vivaldi, *The Four Seasons*, op. 8, no. 1/I, mm. 1-13 (Ritornello theme).

Poetic image: The joyful arrival of spring

Musical depiction: Major key, spirited rhythmic figures, bright character, dance-like quality

Ex. 2.2 Vivaldi, *The Four Seasons*, op. 8, no. 1/I, mm. 13-15.

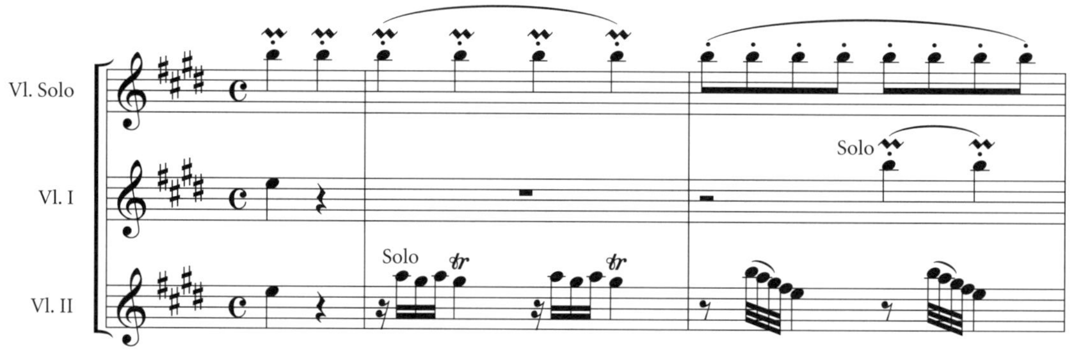

Poetic image ______________________________

Musical depiction ______________________________

____

Ex. 2.3 Vivaldi, *The Four Seasons*, op. 8, no. 1/I, mm. 31-32.

Poetic image ______________________________

Musical depiction ______________________________

____

Ex. 2.4 Vivaldi, *The Four Seasons*, op. 8, no. 1/I, mm. 44-46.

Poetic image ______________________________

Musical depiction ______________________________

____

Ex. 2.5 Vivaldi, *The Four Seasons*, op. 8, no. 1/II, mm. 1-3.

Poetic image ______________________________

Musical depiction ______________________________

____

Ex. 2.6 Vivaldi, *The Four Seasons*, op. 8, no. 1/III, mm. 1-3.

Poetic image ______________________________

Musical depiction ______________________________

____

After listening to a complete performance of *Spring*, summarize your observations by completing the chart below:

Musical Feature	**First Movement**	**Second Movement**	**Third Movement**
Tempo			
Key			
Meter			
Form			
Poetic images and their musical depiction			
Other observations (dynamics, ornamentation, continuo instruments, etc.)			

DID YOU KNOW?

Vivaldi's music fell into relative obscurity after his death. Fortunately, by the mid-20th century a large number of manuscripts that had languished in private collections came to public light. With the advent of the LP (long-playing record) many of these works were recorded and found a receptive audience. Today Vivaldi has been restored to his rightful place in the pantheon of Baroque masters.

Recommended Listening for Vivaldi:
The Four Seasons, op. 8 (*Summer, Autumn, Winter*)
Concerto for Four Violins in B Minor, op. 3, no. 10
"Domini Deus" from *Gloria in D Major*, RV 589

Bach and *The Well-Tempered Clavier*

The Life and Music of Johann Sebastian Bach (1685–1750)

UNIT TWO

The Bach family provided generations of musicians to Northern Germany, but the best-known and most-respected family member was Johann Sebastian. His music represents the ultimate in Baroque craftsmanship and the culmination of hundreds of years of polyphonic writing. He passed on this legacy to his own children, several of whom had successful musical careers. Although Bach did not invent any new genres, he perfected the existing forms of his day while absorbing international influences. A devout Lutheran, Bach dedicated all his works "to the Glory of God."

Explain Bach's connection to the following people and places from his early years:

Eisenach ______________________________

Ohrdruf ______________________________

Arnstadt ______________________________

Maria Barbara ______________________________

C.P.E. Bach ______________________________

W.F. Bach ______________________________

Mühlhausen ______________________________

G.P. Telemann ______________________________

Bach's career is normally divided into three periods based on where he lived and worked. Fill in the requested information for each stage of his career below:

Weimar (______–______)

Patron ______________________________

Responsibilities ______________________________

____

____

Important compositions ______________________________

____

____

Cothen (______–______)

Patron ______________________________

Responsibilities ______________________________

____

____

Important compositions ______________________________

____

____

Anna Magdalena ______________________________

____

Johann Christian Bach ______________________________

Johann Christoph Bach ______________________________

Leipzig (______–______)

Patron ______________________________

Responsibilities ______________________________

____

____

Important compositions ______________________________

____

____

C.P.E. Bach and Frederick the Great ______________________________

____

____

The music of J.S. Bach represents a high point in over one hundred years of Baroque musical practice. Bach's personal style synthesized the leading musical developments in his time. Elaborate on the significant style features below and name two specific Bach compositions for each:

comprehensive approach to large forms ______________________________

____

____

____

1. ______________________ 2. ______________________

contrapuntal mastery ____

____

____

____

1. ______________________ 2. ______________________

Italian influence ____

____

1. ______________________ 2. ______________________

French influence ____

____

1. ______________________ 2. ______________________

English influence ____

____

1. ______________________ 2. ______________________

religious inspiration ____

____

____

____

1. ______________________ 2. ______________________

harmonic language ____

____

____

____

1. ______________________ 2. ______________________

technical challenges ______________________________

____

____

____

1. ______________________ 2. ______________________

DID YOU KNOW? The complete works of J.S. Bach were catalogued by Wolfgang Schmieder and are referred to by BWV numbers (*Bach-Werke-Verzeichnis*).

Building a Musical Vocabulary: *Baroque Counterpoint*

Match each term to the appropriate definition below:

answer	episode	prelude
augmentation	fugue	stretto
countersubject	inversion	subject
diminution	pedal point	tierce de Picardie

______________ In the Baroque era, a short, keyboard work in improvisatory style, usually preceding a fugue.

______________ A highly structured, imitative contrapuntal composition in which a single theme or subject prevails.

______________ The initial statement of the main theme of a fugue in the tonic key.

______________ The second statement of the main theme in a fugue, usually in the dominant key.

______________ A recurring counter-melody accompanying entries of the subject and answer.

______________ A passage within a fugue, frequently sequential, in which neither subject nor answer is present.

______________ Overlapping subject entries in close succession. From the Italian *stringere*, meaning "to tighten."

______________ The presentation of thematic material in longer time values.

______________ The presentation of thematic material in shorter time values.

______________ The presentation of thematic material "upside down."

______________ A common mannerism of ending a minor key work in the tonic major (raised third).

______________ A sustained note over which harmonies change.

Supplemental Activity: *Identifying Fugal Answers*

In a fugue, the answer may be either tonal or real. A *real* answer is an exact transposition of the subject. In a *tonal* answer, one or more of the intervals are adjusted to accommodate the harmony.

In the musical excerpts below, identify each of the answers as tonal or real:

Ex. 2.7 Bach, *The Well-Tempered Clavier*, Vol. 1, No. 6 in D Minor

❑ Real Answer ❑ Tonal

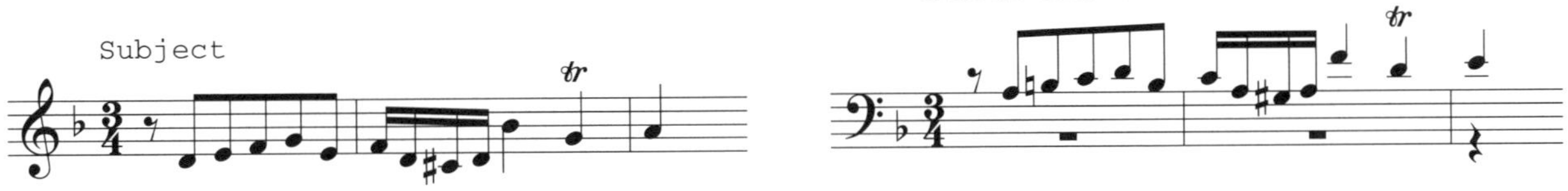

Ex. 2.8 Bach, *The Well-Tempered Clavier*, Vol. 1, No. 21 in B flat Major

❑ Real Answer ❑ Tonal

Ex. 2.9 Bach, *The Well-Tempered Clavier*, Vol. 1, No. 5 in D Major

❑ Real Answer ❑ Tonal Answer

Ex. 2.10 Bach, *The Well-Tempered Clavier*, Vol. 1, No. 16 in G Minor

❑ Real Answer ❑ Tonal Answer

DID YOU KNOW? DID YOU KNOW?

The infamous "lost son of Bach," otherwise known as P.D.Q. Bach (1807–1742), sprang from the fertile imagination of American musicologist Peter Schickele. Works attributed to this fictitious composer parody classical music traditions and Baroque musical style. On the compact disc, "P.D.Q. Bach: The Short-Tempered Clavier and Other Dysfunctional Works for Keyboard," Schickele included Preludes and Fugues in all the major and minor keys "Except for the Really Hard Ones."

Required Listening: *The Well-Tempered Clavier*

The Well-Tempered Clavier demonstrates a craftsmanship bordering on wizardry. Bach employed a vast array of contrapuntal devices and approaches throughout both volumes, and there is great variety from one piece to the next. This work is an enduring and monumental contribution to the keyboard literature.

What is the German title of this collection?

____

In Bach's day, what did the words *Well-Tempered* and *Clavier* signify?

Well-Tempered ________________________________

Clavier ________________________________

How many volumes comprise *The Well-Tempered Clavier*? ____________

What does each volume contain? ________________________________

____

What is the key scheme in each volume? ________________________________

____

____

Choose **ONE Prelude and Fugue** from either volume of *The Well-Tempered Clavier*. Study the score while listening to a recording of your choice, then summarize your observations by filling in the charts below:

Prelude and Fugue No. ______ Volume ______ Key ______ Meter ______

Recording: Artist ____________________

Instrument ____________________

Prelude

Formal Structure (if applicable)	
Texture	
Principal Modulations	
Rhythmic Character	
Predominant Affection	
Special Features	

Fugue

Fugue Subject (notate on staff)	
Number of Voices	
Type of Fugue Answer	☐ Real ☐ Tonal
Countersubject(s)	☐ None ☐ 1 ☐ 2
Principal Modulations	
Elements present (check all that apply) ☐ Episodes ☐ Inversion ☐ Augmentation ☐ Diminution ☐ Stretto (indicate measure numbers) ____________ ☐ Voice splitting ☐ Pedal point ☐ Tierce de Picardie ☐ Other	
Underlying Affection	

Recommended Listening for J.S. Bach:
Brandenburg Concerto No. 5, BWV 1050
Italian Concerto, BWV 971
Cantata No. 140 "Wachet auf," BWV 140
Concerto for Four Harpsichords in A Minor (transcribed after Vivaldi), BWV 1065
Selections from the *Anna Magdalena Notebook*
Organ Toccata and Fugue in D Minor, BWV 565

Bach Works in the *Celebration Series Perspectives®*:
Invention No. 1 in C Major, BWV 772 (*Piano Repertoire 7*)
Little Prelude in D Major, BWV 925 (*Piano Repertoire 8*)
Invention No. 13 in A Minor, BWV 784 (*Piano Repertoire 8*)
Sinfonia No. 7 in E Minor, BWV 793 (*Piano Repertoire 9*)
Sinfonia No. 6 in E Major, BWV 792 (*Piano Repertoire 9*)
Prelude and Fugue in C Minor, BWV 847 (*Piano Repertoire 9*)
Fantasia in C Minor, BWV 906 (*Piano Repertoire 10*)
French Suite No. 5, BWV 816: Allemande and Gigue (*Piano Repertoire 10*)
Prelude and Fugue in E Flat Major, BWV 876 (*Piano Repertoire 10*)

Handel and *Messiah*

The Life and Music of George Frideric Handel (1685–1759)

Handel's life and career exemplify the cosmopolitan spirit of the Baroque period. A virtuoso organist and violinist, an esteemed conductor and a versatile composer, he absorbed aspects of German, Italian, French, and English styles. This international awareness led him to Italian opera, which for a time was the central focus of his creative work. Even as he moved on to explore other genres, Handel's operatic style remained intrinsic to his music.

Explain Handel's connection to the following people and places:

Halle ______________________________

Hamburg ______________________________

____

Italy ______________________________

____

____

____

Hanover ______________________________

____

London ______________________________

____

____

____

Describe the unexpected turn of events that transpired upon the death of Queen Anne in 1712.

____

____

____

For what purpose was the Royal Academy of Music formed and what was Handel's association with that institution?

____

____

____

____

Who were some of the leading singers engaged by Handel?

____

What factors contributed to the demise of the Royal Academy of Music?

____

____

____

____

Describe the personal hardships Handel suffered in his life and career.

____

____

____

____

Where was Handel laid to rest? _______________

Define the following genres and name two Handel compositions for each:

Orchestral suite _______________

____

____

1. _______________ 2. _______________

Opera seria _______________

____

____

1. _______________ 2. _______________

Oratorio _______________

____

____

1. _______________ 2. _______________

DID YOU KNOW? DID YOU KNOW?

Although Bach and Handel never met, both composers sought treatment for their failing eyesight from John Taylor, a self-promoting doctor with an unsavory reputation. In 1749, Taylor operated on Bach's eyes twice, but afterward Bach's blindness was total and his health began to fail (he died within the year). In 1751, Handel submitted to Taylor's knife, and he too came out of the surgery without improvement.

Building a Musical Vocabulary: *Oratorio*

Define the following as they relate to oratorio:

French overture

word painting

recitativo secco

recitativo accompagnato

da capo aria

melisma

libretto

Required Listening: Selections from *Messiah*

The audience in attendance on April 13, 1742 at Neale's Music Hall in Dublin could not have guessed that the work they were about to hear would come to enjoy a popularity and recognition that few other compositions can match. With its French overture, Italianate recitatives and arias, Germanic counterpoint, and rich English choral writing, *Messiah* stands as a testament to the internationalism of its composer and its era.

Answer the following questions about *Messiah* by circling the letter next to the correct response:

What genre does *Messiah* represent?

a) *opera seria*
b) masque
c) oratorio

To whom were the proceeds of the first performance given?

a) Handel himself
b) George I
c) local charities

Who was the librettist for this work?

a) Charles Jennens
b) John Milton
c) Nahum Tate

The libretto was based on passages from:

a) the Old Testament
b) the New Testament
c) both Old and New Testaments

How did the text for *Messiah* differ from the texts of most of Handel's oratorios?

a) it was written in prose
b) it was made up entirely of rhyming couplets
c) it was composed in sonnet form

In which language was this work written?

a) German
b) English
c) Italian

By all accounts, how long did it take Handel to compose the music?

a) 24 days
b) 24 weeks
c) 24 months

What orchestration did Handel employ?

a) strings and continuo
b) oboes, bassoons, trumpets, and timpani
c) all of the above

What vocal forces does this work require?

a) SATB chorus and SATB soloists
b) SATB chorus but no soloists
c) SATB soloists without any chorus

What is the theme of Part One?

a) the prophesy of the coming of Christ and his birth
b) Christ's suffering, death, and the spread of his doctrine
c) the redemption of the world through faith

What is the theme of Part Two?

a) the prophesy of the coming of Christ and his birth
b) Christ's suffering, death, and the spread of his doctrine
c) the redemption of the world through faith

What is the theme of Part Three?

a) the prophesy of the coming of Christ and his birth
b) Christ's suffering, death, and the spread of his doctrine
c) the redemption of the world through faith

Overture to *Messiah*

Listen to a recording of the *Messiah* Overture. If possible, follow a score while you listen. Describe the Overture by completing the outline below:

Title (as identified in the score) "____________________"

Genre ______________ overture   Musical form ____________________

Key ____________________   Time signature __________________

Section A

Ex. 2.11 Handel, *Messiah*, Overture, mm. 1-4.

Tempo ______________ Texture ______________

Predominant rhythm ______________

What atmosphere is created? ______________

Section B: Fugue

Ex. 2.12 Handel, *Messiah*, Overture, mm. 13-20.

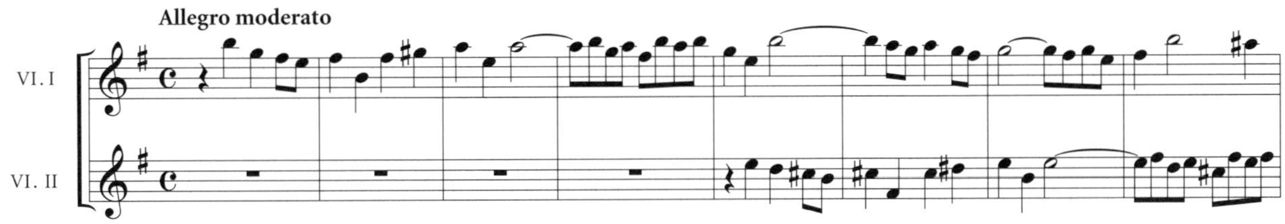

Tempo ______________ Texture ______________

Number of voices ______________

Subject introduced by ______________

Answer: Real or tonal? ______________

Selections from *Messiah* (Student's Choice)

Choose **ONE recitative, ONE aria,** and **ONE chorus** from *Messiah.* Listen to a recording. If possible, follow a score while you listen. For each selection, record your observations by completing the outlines below:

Recitative

Title ______________

Full text ______________

____

____

____

Voice type ______________

Type of recitative ______________

General description ______________

____

____

____

Aria

Title ______________________________

On the staff below, write out the first four measures of the melody line from the aria you have chosen.

Full text ______________________________

____

____

____

Voice type ______________ Key ______________

Meter ______________ Tempo ______________

Form (if applicable): ______________________________

Describe the following musical features for the aria you have chosen:

Introduction ______________________________

____

Melody ______________________________

____

Accompaniment ______________________________

____

Harmony/key structure ______________________________

____

Word painting ______________________________

____

Postlude/coda ______________________________

____

Overall atmosphere/underlying affection ______________________________

____

Chorus

Title ____________________

Full text ____________________

____

____

____

Key ______ Meter ______ Tempo ____________________

Describe the following musical features for the chorus you have chosen:

Introduction ____________________

____

Melody ____________________

____

Harmony/key structure ____________________

____

Texture(s) ____________________

____

Accompaniment ____________________

____

Word painting ____________________

____

Postlude/coda ____________________

____

Overall atmosphere/underlying affection ____________________

____

In London, the 18th-century house where Handel lived for 36 years became a museum in November 2001. Working from Handel's will and an inventory of the house made after his death, museum workers restored the upper floors at 25 Brook Street to the condition they were in when Handel lived there. Interestingly, the house next door, which is also part of the museum, is where rock star Jimi Hendrix lived from 1968-1969.

Recommended Listening for Handel:

Selections from *Water Music*, HWV 348-350
Selections from *Music for the Royal Fireworks*, HWV 351
"Arrival of the Queen of Sheba" from *Solomon*, HWV 67
"Harmonious Blacksmith" from *Clavier Suite No. 5*, HWV 430

Handel Works in *Celebration Series Perspectives®*:
Suite No. 8 in G Major, HWV 441: Aria (*Piano Repertoire 7*)
Suite No. 7 in G Minor, HWV 432: Gigue (*Piano Repertoire 8)*
Suite No. 4 in E Minor, HWV 429: Allemande (*Piano Repertoire 9*)

Supplemental Activity: *Putting Baroque Composers on the Map*

On the map below, find the cities where Vivaldi, Bach, and Handel lived and worked during their careers. Highlight the cities where Vivaldi resided with red dots, Bach with blue dots, and Handel with green dots.

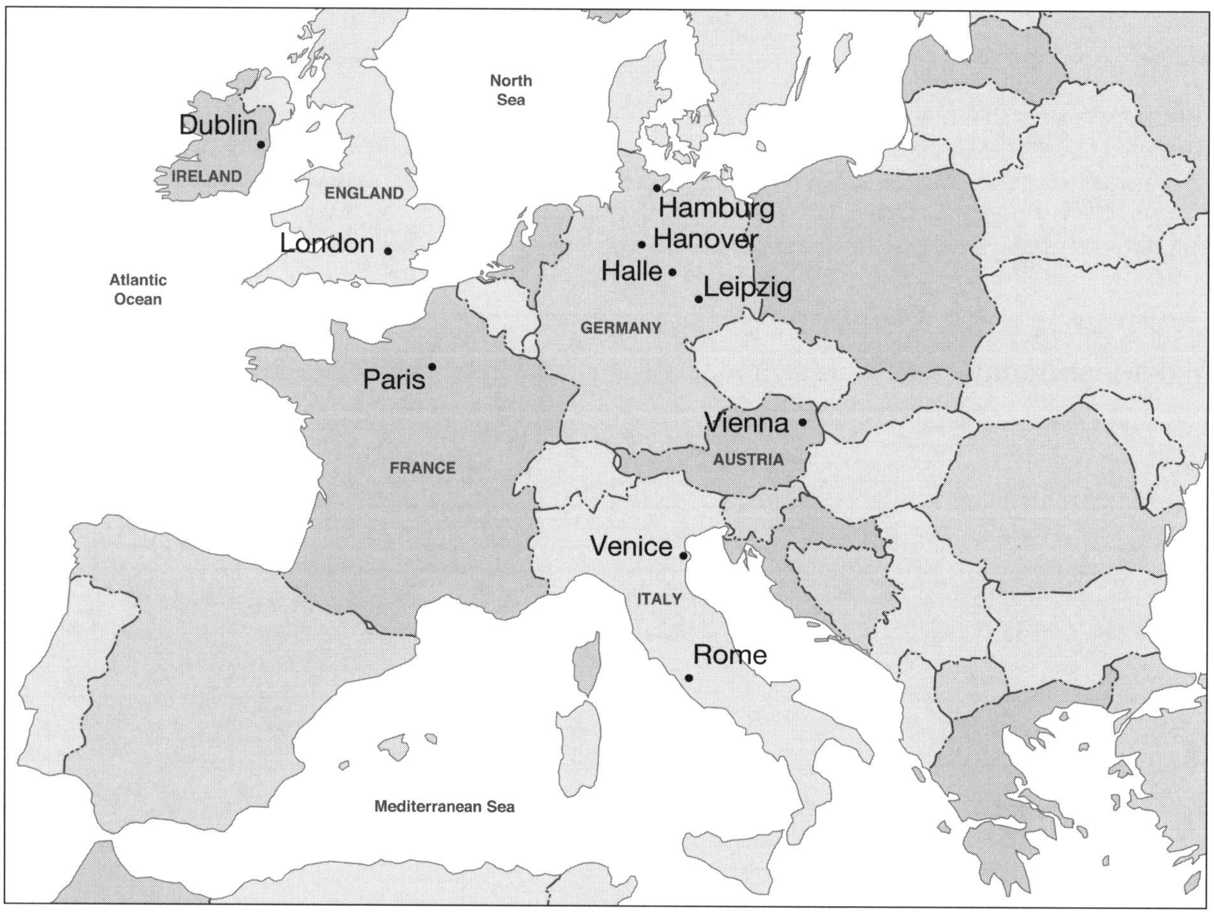

WEB QUEST

Be a "virtual tourist" and visit some of the cities, churches, and homes where Vivaldi, Bach, and Handel lived and worked. Using a search engine, combine the names of the composers with the appropriate city. Try additional words like *museum, house, birthplace (Geburtshaus), monuments, tours,* etc.

Compare the musical careers of Vivaldi, Bach, and Handel by completing the chart below:

	Vivaldi	**Bach**	**Handel**
Dates	________	________	________
Birthplace	________	________	________
Education	________	________	________
	________	________	________
Instruments played	________	________	________
	________	________	________
Travels	________	________	________
	________	________	________
Places of employment and/or patrons	________	________	________
	________	________	________
	________	________	________
	________	________	________
Genres cultivated	________	________	________
	________	________	________
	________	________	________
	________	________	________
	________	________	________
Hallmarks of individual style	________	________	________
	________	________	________
	________	________	________
	________	________	________
	________	________	________

Review and Reflection

What do *you* like about Baroque musical style? Do you have a favorite composer or piece? Of the works you studied in this unit, which did you enjoy the most, and why?

____

____

____

____

____

____

____

____

Quiz

Name the composers to which each of the following statements best applies:

1. Fully developed the Baroque fugue. ____________
2. Cultivated *opera seria* in London. ____________
3. Developed the Italian solo violin concerto. ____________
4. Compositions dedicated "to the glory of God." ____________
5. Continued the family legacy of professional music-making. ____________
6. Worked for the English monarchy. ____________
7. Conducted a girls' orchestra. ____________
8. Involved in the selection and improvement of church organs. ____________
9. Shifted compositional focus from opera to oratorio. ____________
10. Responsible for the musical activities of four churches in Leipzig. ____________

UNIT THREE

THE CLASSICAL PERIOD (*ca* 1750–*ca* 1825)

Historians often refer to the late 18th century as the Age of Enlightenment. This was an era characterized by the pursuit of knowledge, rational thinking, and a growing—and controversial—desire for equality amongst all people. While Italy was the center of musical activity in the Baroque era, the city of Vienna took on this role in the Classical period. Ironically, not one of the three great giants of the "Viennese School" (Haydn, Mozart, and Beethoven) was a native son, yet all were drawn to the city by its vibrant culture and patronage of the arts.

The Classical ideals of proportion, symmetry, and balance are present in the art and music of the late 18th century. Having rediscovered the simplicity and clean lines of Greco-Roman art, artists and architects began to move away from the ornate style that was popular in the Baroque period. Of the many musical developments that took place, the emergence of sonata form, with its focus on structural balance, stands out as the defining achievement of the Classical period.

Before we embark on our exploration of Classical music, you should have an overview of the cultural and historical events of the time. Examine the timeline below to see how many people and events you recognize. In the space provided, add four additional events or people of interest to you.

Timeline

1750 – 1825

Historical Events	• **1752** Benjamin Franklin discovers electricity; • **1769** James Watt invents steam engine; • **1776** American Declaration of Independence; • **1789** French Revolution launched; • **1793** The Louvre established as public art gallery; • **1812** Napoleon invades Russia; • **1816** Stethoscope invented Photography born
Important Figures	**Jean Jacques Rousseau** 1712–1778; **Johann Wolfgang von Goethe** 1749–1832; **E.T.A. Hoffman** 1756–1822; **Friedrich Schiller** 1759–1796
Composers	**G.B. Sammartini** 1701–1775; **C.W. Gluck** 1714–1787; **C.P.E. Bach** 1714–1788; **Franz Joseph Haydn** 1732–1809; **Karl Stamitz** 1745–1801; **Muzio Clementi** 1752–1832; **Wolfgang Amadeus Mozart** 1756–1791; **Ludwig van Beethoven** 1770–1827
Additional Events/People	

Historical and Cultural Background

Explain the origins of the term "classical."

List eight words that apply to the Classical spirit:

Circle two other names by which this historical period is known:

Age of Reason	Dark Ages
Ars Nova	Age of Absolute Monarchy
Age of Enlightenment	

Explain the concept of *patronage of the arts* as it existed in the Classical period.

Name some of the historical events and cultural figures that shaped this era:

Historical events 1. ______

2. ______

3. ______

Monarchs 1. ______________________

2. ______________________

Philosophers 1. ______________________

2. ______________________

Writers 1. ______________________

2. ______________________

Artists 1. ______________________

2. ______________________

UNIT THREE

Building a Musical Vocabulary: *Elements of Classical Style*

Define the following terms as they apply to Classical musical style:

absolute music ______________________

sonata cycle (multi-movement structure) ______________________

menuet and trio ______________________

scherzo and trio ______________________

theme and variations ______________________

rondo ______________________

sonata-rondo ______________________________

____

____

symmetrical phrasing ______________________________

____

diatonic harmony ______________________________

____

Alberti bass ______________________________

____

rocket theme ______________________________

____

open cadence ______________________________

____

closed cadence ______________________________

____

____

Sonata-Allegro Form

The most important musical structure to evolve in the Classical period was Sonata-Allegro form. Also known as first movement form, or simply sonata form, Sonata-Allegro form developed from the *rounded-binary* principle. This came about through the efforts of Pre-Classical composers such as Carl Philipp Emanuel Bach, Johann Christian Bach, and Karl Stamitz, as well as composers of the Viennese School.

Ex. 3.1 Rounded Binary Diagram

Section A	:‖:	Section B	+	Section A	:‖
Open cadence Modulates to Dominant or Relative Major				Return of the opening, usually altered to stay in Tonic Key	

The structure shown in Ex. 3.1 evolved into the expanded two-part form shown in Ex. 3.2. It contains the Exposition–Development–Recapitulation design that served as a template for individual movements within the sonata cycle.

Ex. 3.2 Sonata-Allegro Form Diagram

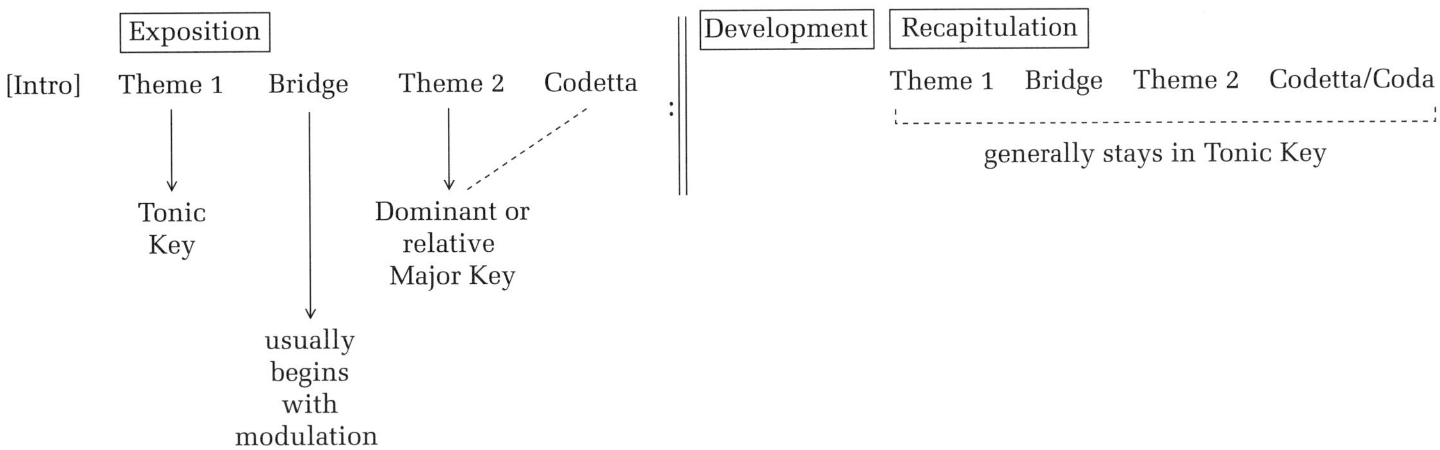

List the events that unfold in each of the principal sections of a typical Sonata-Allegro form. Answers to the first few sections have been provided as models.

Introduction (optional) Usually slow; not always related to what comes later; establishes tonic key, though sometimes in tonic major/minor; creates musical tension and suspense to capture listeners' attention.

Exposition

First theme Establishes tonic key; presents distinct melodic idea; striking rhythmic character; often sets tone and mood for the entire movement.

Bridge Initiates move to new key center; often consists of scale figurations or chordal passages.

Second theme __________

Codetta __________

Development

Recapitulation

First theme

Bridge

Second theme

Codetta

Coda

Listening For Elements of Classical Style

Part One:
Listen to a recording of the first movement from Mozart's famous *Sonata in C Major*, K 545.

1. Referring to the Classical style elements you defined on pp. 53-54, identify the musical features that are present in this piece.

2. Examine a score for this sonata movement. With your teacher's help, complete a simple analysis, identifying the main structural elements of sonata form.

Part Two:
From your own repertoire, identify one work from the Classical era. Compile a list of the musical features that apply to your piece:

Title

Composer

Instrument

Musical features

If you are a piano student, you have probably played many *sonatinas* by composers including Clementi, Kuhlau, and Diabelli. Sonatinas are miniature versions of sonatas, as the suffix "ina" indicates. They typically have a multi-movement structure, and the first-movements are usually small-scale Sonata-Allegro forms.

Haydn and the String Quartet

The Life and Music of Franz Joseph Haydn (1732–1809)

Often regarded as the father of Classical style, "Papa" Haydn was a key figure in the development of the symphony, sonata, and string quartet. During his long and prolific career, Haydn enjoyed the benefits of the patronage system. Having the same employer for many years allowed him to experiment with approaches to formal structure and instrumental writing. Haydn's music incorporates a wide range of elements: robust energy, the spirit of folk music, wit, and humor. Toward the end of his life, both Mozart and Beethoven paid him homage, acknowledging their musical debt to this great Classical master.

Explain Haydn's connection to the following people and places:

Rohrau ______________________________

Vienna ______________________________

____

St. Stephen's Cathedral ______________________________

____

Michael and Johann Haydn ______________________________

____

The Esterházy family ______________________________

____

____

____

Mozart ______________________________

____

Paris ______________________________

____

London ______________________________

____

____

____

Oxford University ______________________________

____

Beethoven ______________________________

____

What duties and obligations did Haydn fulfill while in the service of the Esterházy family? How did the patronage system affect his career?

____

____

____

____

For each of the following genres, list Haydn's contributions and innovations. Identify representative works for each category. Include descriptive titles for works that have them.

symphony Over 100 symphonies, including No. 94 "Surprise," No. 100 "Military," No. 104 "London"

keyboard sonata ______________________________

____

string quartet ______________________________

____

oratorio ______________________________

____

opera ______________________________

____

mass ______________________________

____

concerto ______________________________

____

Comment on the following aspects of Haydn's musical style:

formal structure ______________________________

____

____

folk elements ______________________________

____

____

humor ______________________________

____

____

dramatic elements ______________________________

____

____

other ______________________________

____

____

Required Listening: *Selected String Quartets*

Listen to a recording of **EITHER** the fourth movement of *Quartet in D Minor*, op. 76, no. 2 **OR** the second movement of *Quartet in C Major*, op. 76, no. 3. If possible, follow a score while you listen. Answer the questions and complete the required outline for the quartet you have chosen.

String Quartet in D Minor, op. 76, no. 2 "Quinten"

How many movements are in this quartet? ______________

The excerpt in Ex. 3.3 is from the first movement. What feature of the motive makes the nickname "Quinten" appropriate?

____

Ex. 3.3 Haydn, *Quartet*, op. 76, no. 2/I, mm. 1-2.

By what name is the third movement referred to? ______________________

Suggest a reason for this designation. ______________________

____

____

Fourth Movement

Key ______________________ Form ______________________

Tempo ______________________ Meter ______________________

Exposition

First Theme

Ex. 3.4 Haydn, *Quartet*, op. 76, no. 2/IV, mm. 1-8.

Describe the character/mood of the first theme. ______________________

____

What rhythmic devices help to establish this mood? ______________________

____

Bridge

Ex. 3.5 Haydn, *Quartet*, op. 76, no. 2/IV, mm. 22-25.

The bridge grows out of the first theme. Which instrument has taken over this theme from the first violin? ____________________

Second Theme Group

Ex. 3.6 Haydn, *Quartet*, op. 76, no. 2/IV, mm. 50-56.

Ex. 3.7 Haydn, *Quartet*, op. 76, no. 2/IV, mm. 63-70.

New key: ______ Relationship to home key: ____________________

How does the second theme group contrast with the opening theme?

____

____

____

***Codetta* (mm. 83-92)**

The codetta confirms the ________________ key and uses a ____________ pedal point.

The exposition is not repeated, as there is no repeat sign in the score. Can you think of any reasons why Haydn might have chosen not to include a repeat?

____

Development

What thematic material forms the basis for the development section and how is it treated?

____

____

How is the texture varied?

____

____

Recapitulation

First Theme

How has the first theme been altered?

____

____

Bridge

As in the exposition, the bridge in the recapitulation grows out of the first theme.

In what key is it now played? _____ Major

In this passage, only three instruments are employed. Which instrument is not playing? ________________

Second Theme Group

Identify the key. ________________

Coda (m. 243)

Through what means does Haydn create a dramatic conclusion to the movement?

____

____

____

String Quartet in C Major, op. 76, no. 3 "Emperor"

How many movements are in this quartet? ____________________

Why is this quartet referred to as the "Emperor"?

____

____

What is the German subtitle for this quartet? ____________________

UNIT THREE

Second Movement

Key ____________________ Form ____________________

Tempo ____________________ Meter ____________________

On which tune is this movement based? ____________________

____

What prompted Haydn to compose this melody and when was it first sung?

____

____

Theme

Ex. 3.8 Haydn, *Quartet*, op. 76, no. 2/II, mm. 1-20.

What mood does Haydn create in this movement and through what means?

____

____

____

Does the internal form of the theme in Ex. 3.8 suggest binary or ternary form?

____

Complete the chart below:

Section	Instrument that plays the theme	Character of this section
Variation 1		
Variation 2		
Variation 3		
Variation 4		

What are the musical elements that firmly ground this movement in the Classical style?

____

____

____

Recommended Listening for Haydn:
Symphony No. 94, Hob. I:94 ("Surprise"), Second Movement
Piano Sonata No. 53 in E Minor, Hob. XVI:34
"The Representation of Chaos," "In Splendor Bright," and "The Heavens are Telling" from *The Creation*, Hob. XXI:2

Haydn Works in *Celebration Series Perspectives®*:
Sonata in D Major, Hob. XVII: D1/III (*Piano Repertoire 7*)
Sonata in G Major, Hob. XVI: 39/I (*Piano Repertoire 8)*
Sonata in E Minor, Hob. XVI:34 (complete) (*Piano Repertoire 9*)
Sonata in D Major, Hob. XVI: 33 (complete) (*Piano Repertoire 10*)

Mozart and *Eine kleine Nachtmusik*

The Life and Music of Wolfgang Amadeus Mozart (1756–1791)

Mozart is possibly the most cherished of all Classical musical figures. The most celebrated child prodigy of all time, he had performed for royalty before the age of six, and by his early teens he had composed operas, solo keyboard works, chamber music, and symphonies. Unlike Haydn, Mozart struggled with the constraints of the patronage system throughout his career.

The lyricism that Mozart cultivated in his operas found expression in virtually every other genre he explored. Because of the ease and spontaneity with which he put musical thought to paper, Mozart won the envy and admiration of future composers. When one considers the personal tribulations he encountered and his tragic early death, his achievements become all the more remarkable.

Explain Mozart's connection to the following people and places:

Salzburg

Leopold Mozart

Maria Anna (Nannerl)

Empress Maria Theresa

European tour

Hieronymus von Colloredo

Vienna

Franz Joseph Haydn

Emperor Joseph II

Constanze Weber

Lorenzo da Ponte

Prague

Leopold II ______________________________

____

Order of Freemasons ______________________________

____

Emanuel Schikaneder ______________________________

____

Barbara Ployer & Maria Theresa von Paradis ______________________________

____

F.X. Süssmayr ______________________________

____

Ludwig Koechel ______________________________

____

List six characteristics of Mozart's musical style:

1. Vocal lyricism carried over from opera to his instrumental works.
2. ______________________________
3. ______________________________
4. ______________________________
5. ______________________________
6. ______________________________

Name and define the three types of opera that Mozart wrote. Give two examples of each:

1. Type ______________________________

   Definition ______________________________

   ____

   ____

   Examples 1. ______________ 2. ______________

UNIT THREE

2. Type ____________________

Definition ____________________

____

Examples 1. ______________ 2. ______________

3. Type ____________________

Definition ____________________

____

Examples 1. ______________ 2. ______________

Name two compositions by Mozart for each of the following genres:

Choral works ______________ ______________

Keyboard works ______________ ______________

Chamber music ______________ ______________

Symphonies ______________ ______________

Required Listening: *Eine kleine Nachtmusik,* K 525

This famous and charming serenade for strings by Mozart serves as an excellent introduction to the Classical sonata cycle. Composed in 1787, it was intended to serve as light entertainment for an aristocratic audience. Symmetrical phrases, essentially diatonic harmony, and clarity of texture are characteristic features.

What is the English title of this work? ____________________

What genre does it represent? ____________________

For which instruments was this work likely intended?

____

First Movement

Key ______________ Form ______________

Tempo ______________ Meter ______________

Review the model of Sonata-Allegro form presented on p. 55 before filling in the following blanks.

Exposition

First Theme

Ex. 3.9 Mozart, *Eine kleine Nachtmusik*, K 525/I, mm. 1-4.

How does the opening melody capture the attention of the listener?

____

What term is used to describe the melodic contours of the first theme?

____

What harmonic progression is used in the excerpt above to establish the tonic key?

_______ – _______

Bridge

Ex. 3.10 Mozart, *Eine kleine Nachtmusik*, K 525/I, mm. 18-21.

Which instrument carries the melodic line in the bridge? ____________________

How is this melody constructed? ______________________________________

____

____

In Ex. 3.10, circle the note that provides the first clue that a modulation to the dominant key is taking place.

Second Theme Group (Principal Theme)

Ex. 3.11 Mozart, *Eine kleine Nachtmusik*, K 525/I, mm. 28-31.

Mozart frequently creates striking contrast between first and second themes in his expositions. Comparing the excerpts in Ex. 3.9 and 3.11, consider how he achieves contrast in this case.

New key ______________________

Melodic contour ____

Dynamic indication ____

Rhythm ____

In the expositions of many Sonata-Allegro movements, the second theme area may be extended with a secondary or subsidiary theme. This extra theme gives the composer more time to establish the new key convincingly. This Mozart movement contains a secondary theme in the new key.

Second Theme Group (Secondary Theme)

Ex. 3.12 Mozart, *Eine kleine Nachtmusik*, K 525/I, mm. 35-38.

How is the insistent quality of the secondary theme achieved musically?

____

____

Codetta

Ex. 3.13 Mozart, *Eine kleine Nachtmusik*, K 525/I, mm. 51-55.

How does the codetta reinforce and solidify the dominant key?

____

____

Development

Opening key ______________________

Identify which themes from the exposition appear in this section, and describe how they are treated.

____

____

____

In Sonata-Allegro form, towards the end of the development there is typically a strong emphasis on the dominant chord, which prepares the listener for the return of the main theme in the tonic key. This musical event is referred to as *dominant preparation*. In this particular movement, the dominant preparation occurs in mm. 70-75 but there is an unexpected twist. Which key does the passage in Ex. 3.14 seem to be hinting at? ____________________

Ex. 3.14 Mozart, *Eine kleine Nachtmusik*, K 525/I, mm. 70-75.

Recapitulation

Compare the musical events of the recapitulation with those of the exposition. What remains the same, and what is different or omitted?

____

____

____

____

Coda

What thematic material is used in the Coda?

____

____

____

American humorist and radio personality Garrison Keilor teamed up with American mezzo-soprano Frederica von Stade to produce the recording *"Songs of the Cat."* One of the featured tracks is a delightful parody of the first movement of *Eine kleine Nachtmusik*, entitled *"Eine kleine Kat."*

Second Movement ("Romanza")

Key ____________________ Form ____________________

Tempo ____________________ Meter ____________________

How is the key of this movement related to the key of the first movement?

Section A

Ex. 3.15 Mozart, *Eine kleine Nachtmusik*, K 525/II, mm. 1-4.

How are the ideals of Classical balance, proportion, and elegance achieved in this opening theme?

Within the A section, what small-scale form does Mozart use as an internal structure?

a) rounded-binary form

b) theme and variations

c) ternary form

Section B

Ex. 3.16 Mozart, *Eine kleine Nachtmusik*, K 525/II, mm. 17-20.

How does this section contrast with the opening?

Return of Section A

The A section is restated in mm. 31-38. Is this an exact repetition of the first statement? ______________________

Section C

Ex. 3.17 Mozart, *Eine kleine Nachtmusik*, K 525/II, mm. 39-42.

What is the new key? ______

How is this key related to the home key? ______________

What device does Mozart use to create a more agitated mood here?

a) a pedal point in the cello line
b) insistent repeated-note figures in the second violins and violas
c) arpeggios in the first violins

What does the texture in this section include?

a) an imitative dialogue between first violins and cellos
b) first and second violins playing melodic lines in unison
c) blocked chords

Return of Section A (m. 51)

Coda **(m. 67)**
What is the origin of the material in the Coda?

a) the first movement
b) Section A of this movement
c) Section C of this movement

Third Movement

Key ______________ Form ______________

Tempo ______________ Meter ______________

Section A (Minuet)

Ex. 3.18 Mozart, *Eine kleine Nachtmusik*, K 525/III, mm. 1-8.

What characteristic features of the minuet are present in this section?

What is the internal structure of this A section?

a) binary form
b) ternary form
c) rondo form

Section B (Trio)

Ex. 3.19 Mozart, *Eine kleine Nachtmusik*, K 525/III, mm. 17-24.

New key ______________ Relationship to the home key ______________

How does the musical character of the Trio section contrast with the Minuet?

Return of Section A

At the end of the Trio (m. 36) the Italian words *"Menuetto da Capo"* appear. What does this indicate to the performers?

a) repeat the trio
b) return to the beginning of the minuet
c) proceed to the next movement

When Section A is played again, which of the following is usually done?

a) the performers observe the repeats
b) the performers ignore the repeats
c) the performers trade instruments

Fourth Movement

Key ____________________ Form ____________________

Tempo ____________________ Meter ____________________

Mozart often concludes his sonata cycle works with spirited, light-hearted finales, and this movement is no exception. It is based on the alternation of two principal themes, shown in Ex. 3.20 and 3.21.

First Theme

Ex. 3.20 Mozart, *Eine kleine Nachtmusik*, K 525/IV, mm. 1-8.

Second Theme

Ex. 3.21 Mozart, *Eine kleine Nachtmusik*, K 525/IV, mm. 16-23.

How do these two themes contrast with one another?

____

____

____

In the second half of m. 57, an unusual modulation occurs:

Ex. 3.22 Mozart, *Eine kleine Nachtmusik*, K 525/IV, mm. 57-61.

What is the unexpected key shown in Ex. 3.22? ____________

How is this key related to the home key?

a) the subdominant
b) the relative minor
c) lowered submediant (♭VI)

Coda (m. 129)
Which of the principal themes is featured in the Coda?

____

What musical elements contribute to the strong sense of conclusion?

____

____

____

The original manuscript of *Eine kleine Nachtmusik* was recovered in 1955. There is evidence that an additional movement existed (another minuet), but apparently it had been torn out. Who removed this movement—and why—is an unsolved mystery.

Recommended Listening for Mozart:
Symphony No. 40 in G Minor, K 550 (First Movement)
Piano Concerto No. 21 in C Major, K 467 (Second Movement)
Violin Sonata in E Minor, K 304
The Magic Flute, K 620 (Act 2: Aria: "Queen of the Night's Revenge")

Mozart Works in *Celebration Series Perspectives®*:
Sonata in C Major, K 330 (300h)/II (*Piano Repertoire 9*)
Fantasia in D Minor, K 397 (385g) (*Piano Repertoire 9*)
Sonata in E flat Major, K 282 (189g) (complete) (*Piano Repertoire 10*)

Beethoven and *Symphony No. 5*

The Life and Music of Ludwig van Beethoven (1770–1827)

In his life and career, Ludwig van Beethoven embraced the spirit and ideals of both the Classical and Romantic eras. Beethoven fully possessed the integrity and idealism of a true artist; in the face of deafness—a devastating fate for a musician—he demonstrated an unfailing spirit and triumph of will. Musically, his innovative approach and originality are unsurpassed, and his legacy cast a giant shadow on the composers of the 19th century. Beethoven's nine symphonies and thirty-two piano sonatas are crowning achievements in their respective genres. When looked at collectively, they demonstrate his stylistic evolution.

Explain Beethoven's connection to the following people and places:

Bonn ______________________________

____

Johann van Beethoven ______________________________

____

____

Christian Neefe ______________________________

____

____

Mozart ______________________________

____

____

Haydn ______________________________

____

____

Vienna ______________________________

____

____

Prince Lichnowsky ______________________________

____

Count Waldstein ______________________________

____

Count Razumowsky ______________________________

____

Prince Lobkowitz ______________________________

____

Heiligenstadt

Napoleon

Karl Beethoven

Carl Czerny

Friedrich Schiller

What hardships did Beethoven endure personally and in his musical career?

DID YOU KNOW?

Before Beethoven was buried, many admirers who viewed the body snipped locks of his hair as keepsakes. One of these locks has survived, and in 1994 several members of the American Beethoven Society purchased it at auction. Scientific tests were conducted on the hair; these tests revealed that Beethoven suffered from lead poisoning, which may have caused his life-long illnesses, affected his personality, and possibly contributed to his death. Russell Marten documented the history of this particular lock of hair in his book, *Beethoven's Hair* (Broadway Books, 2001).

Because Beethoven's compositional style evolved considerably over the course of his lifetime, his music is typically divided into three style periods: early, middle, and late. Writing about Beethoven in 1926, French composer Vincent d'Indy referred to these three stages as the periods of Imitation, Externalization, and Reflection. Complete the chart below to show the evolution of Beethoven's musical style.

Style Period	Characteristics	Representative Works
Early (1782–1802) (Imitation)		
Middle (1803–1815) (Externalization)		
Late (1815–1827) (Reflection)		

For each of the following genres, list Beethoven's contributions and innovations:

solo piano works ______________________________

____

____

concertos ______________________________

____

____

chamber music ______________________________

____

____

opera ______________________________

____

____

UNIT THREE

other vocal works ____

____

____

symphonies ____

____

____

____

Match the correct nickname (subtitle) to the appropriate Beethoven work:

"Appassionata"	"Ghost"	"Pathétique"
"Archduke"	"Hammerklavier"	"Razumovsky"
"Choral"	"Kreutzer"	"Spring"
"Emperor"	"Moonlight"	"Waldstein"
"Eroica"	"Pastoral"	

Early Period

____________________ *Piano Sonata*, op. 13

____________________ *Violin Sonata*, op. 24

____________________ *Piano Sonata*, op. 27

Middle Period

____________________ *Violin Sonata*, op. 47

____________________ *Piano Sonata*, op. 53

____________________ *Symphony No. 3*, op. 55

____________________ *Piano Sonata*, op. 57

____________________ *String Quartet*, op. 59

____________________ *Symphony No. 6*, op. 68

____________________ *Piano Trio*, op. 70, no. 1

____________________ *Piano Concerto No. 5*, op. 73

____________________ *Piano Trio*, op. 97

Late Period

____________________ *Piano Sonata*, op. 106

____________________ *Symphony No. 9*, op. 125

WEB QUEST

Have you read the famous letter Beethoven wrote to his brothers, known as the *Heiligenstadt Testament?* Look on the internet for a complete translation of this moving document and learn from Beethoven himself what he was feeling as he experienced the onset of deafness.

Required Listening: *Symphony No. 5 in C Minor,* op. 67

From its compelling opening motive to its triumphant final cadence, Beethoven's Fifth Symphony is certainly his most recognized and popular composition. Because the famous four-note motive ("three shorts and a long") reappears in various guises in each movement, this symphony is said to exhibit *cyclic structure.*

When did this symphony receive its first performance? ____________________
Is this work from Beethoven's early, middle, or late style period?

____

Listen to a recording of *Symphony No. 5.* If possible, follow a score while you listen. Complete the required listening outline for each movement.

First Movement

Key ______________________ Form ____________________

Tempo ____________________ Meter ____________________

Exposition

First Theme

Ex. 3.23 Beethoven, *Symphony No. 5*, op. 67/I, mm. 1-5.

How is the four-note motive treated in the opening five measures?

____

____

What effect does this have on the listener?

____

____

____

What compositional devices does Beethoven utilize to maintain dramatic tension leading up to the bridge?

____

____

____

Bridge

Ex. 3.24 Beethoven, *Symphony No. 5*, op. 67/I, mm. 59-63.

The bridge is unusually short. From what musical material it derived, and which instruments present it?

____

____

Second Theme

Ex. 3.25 Beethoven, *Symphony No. 5*, op. 67/I, mm. 63-66.

What new key is established at m. 63 and what is its relationship to the home key?

____

Which instruments present the second theme? ____________________

How does this theme contrast with the first theme?

____

____

What reappears in the low strings, this time serving as an accompaniment?

____

____

Codetta (m. 110)

What thematic material dominates this closing passage?

____

Beethoven places repeat signs at the conclusion of the exposition. Was the repeat sign observed in the recording you listened to? ______________________

Development (m. 125)
Describe the treatment of the four-note motive within the development section.

Describe the dynamic range. ______________________

Which other material from the exposition reappears in the development?

How is suspense created as the development draws to a close?

Recapitulation (m. 248)
As expected, the recapitulation re-establishes the home key of C minor. What unusual and unexpected events occur in this section?

***Coda* (m. 398)**
Extended codas are among Beethoven's many innovative contributions to the development of Sonata-Allegro form. How does Beethoven create drama and tension in this coda?

DID YOU KNOW?

Peter Schickele recorded a very creative narration to the first movement of Beethoven's Fifth Symphony. Done in the style of a sports broadcast complete with crowd noise and amusing commentary, it actually presents an insightful analysis of this Sonata-Allegro movement.

Second Movement

Key ____________________ Form ____________________

Tempo ____________________ Meter ____________________

This movement is structured around two themes, shown in Ex. 3.26 and 3.27.

Theme A

Ex. 3.26 Beethoven, *Symphony No. 5*, op. 67/II, mm. 1-8.

Describe Theme A by commenting on the following:

featured instruments ____________________

rhythm ____________________

melodic contours ____________________

articulation ____________________

Theme B

Ex. 3.27 Beethoven, *Symphony No. 5*, op. 67/II, mm. 22-31.

Describe Theme B by commenting on the following:

featured instruments ____________________

rhythm ____________________

melodic contours ____________________

articulation ____________________

How is Theme B related to the principal theme of the first movement?

____

To what key does this theme unexpectedly modulate? ____________________

The variations that follow the two thematic statements are built principally on Theme A. Briefly describe the compositional techniques or devices used in each of the variations:

Variation 1 ____

____

____

Variation 2 ____

____

____

Variation 3 ____

____

____

Variation 4 ____

____

____

Coda ____

____

____

Third Movement

Key ____________________ Form ____________________

Tempo ____________________ Meter ____________________

What traditional dance movement does this scherzo and trio replace?

____

Section A (Scherzo)

Principal Theme

Ex. 3.28 Beethoven, *Symphony No. 5*, op. 67/III, mm. 1-8.

Which family of instruments plays this theme? ______________________
What term is used to describe a theme that outlines a tonic triad in this manner?

____

Secondary Theme

Ex. 3.29 Beethoven, *Symphony No. 5*, op. 67/III, mm. 19-26.

What instruments are featured in the secondary theme? ______________________

What is the new dynamic level? ______________________

To what previous material is this theme related?

____

What is the effect of the frequently used fermatas in this scherzo?

____

____

Section B (Trio)

Ex. 3.30 Beethoven, *Symphony No. 5*, op. 67/III, mm. 141-146.

What is the new key in the trio? ______________________

What is its relationship to the home key? ______________________

Which instruments are featured? What aspect of the instrumentation is unusual?

____

____

Describe the texture. ______________________

____

How does the character of the trio contrast with the scherzo?

____

____

____

UNIT THREE

Return of Section A (m. 236)
How has this been altered from the original statement?

____

____

____

How does Beethoven create suspense at the end of this movement?

____

____

What does the Italian term *attacca* at the end of the scherzo indicate to the performers?

____

____

Fourth Movement

Key ______________ Form ______________

Tempo ______________ Meter ______________

How are the keys of the first and fourth movements related?

____

In this movement, Beethoven makes use of some orchestral instruments that were new at the time. What are they?

______________ ______________ ______________

Exposition

First Theme

Ex. 3.31 Beethoven, *Symphony No. 5*, op. 67/IV, mm. 1-8.

Beethoven uses full orchestra in the opening passage of this movement, conveying a grand, majestic character. What other musical means are used to create this effect?

____

____

____

Bridge

Ex. 3.32 Beethoven, *Symphony No. 5*, op. 67/IV, mm. 1-8.

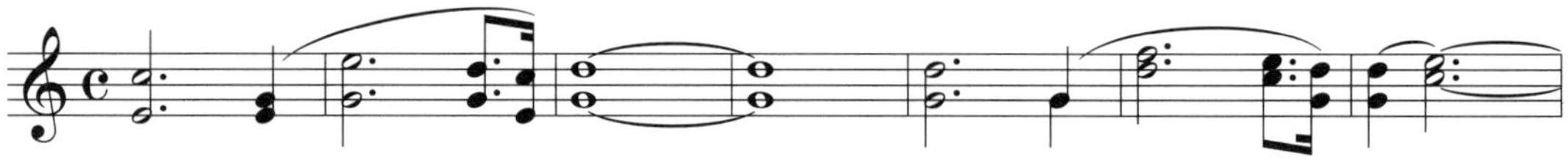

Which instruments are heard most prominently in the bridge?

____

What key is introduced in this section? ____________________

Second Theme

Ex. 3.33 Beethoven, *Symphony No. 5*, op. 67/IV, mm. 45-48.

Describe how this theme contrasts the first theme in terms of the following:

rhythm ______________________________________

texture ______________________________________

melodic contour ______________________________

dynamics ____________________________________

Can you draw any connection between the opening motive of this theme and material heard previously?

____

____

____

Codetta

Ex. 3.34 Beethoven, *Symphony No. 5*, op. 67/IV, mm. 64-71.

Which instruments are featured in the opening of the codetta?

____

Describe the construction of this melody.

____

____

Beethoven places repeat signs at the conclusion of the exposition. Was the repeat sign observed in the recording you listened to? ______________

Development

What thematic material dominates this development and how is it treated?

____

____

____

____

What important material heard earlier in the work makes a final brief appearance in C minor?

____

____

Which instruments present this material? ______________

How is musical tension created in preparation for the recapitulation?

____

Recapitulation

In this recapitulation, comment on which elements remain unchanged and which have been altered.

____

____

____

____

Coda

Of the new instruments Beethoven introduced in this work, which one is highlighted in the Coda? ______________

How is it featured? ______________

How does the length of this Coda compare to what you might expect?

____

At the Presto (m. 362), what material from the exposition reappears?

___

What is the effect of this tempo change?

___

___

At the conclusion of this work, following the final cadence, how many times is the tonic chord repeated? ___

Explain how this symphony demonstrates cyclic structure.

___

___

___

___

___

Summarize the innovations and musical surprises that Beethoven built into this composition.

___

___

___

___

___

___

Recommended Listening for Beethoven:
Symphony No. 9, op. 125, Fourth Movement
Violin Sonata in F Major, op. 24 ("Spring"), First Movement
Piano Concerto No. 5 in E flat Major, op. 73 ("Emperor")
Piano Sonata in C sharp Minor, op. 27, no. 2 ("Moonlight")

Beethoven Works in *Celebration Series Perspectives®*:
Für Elise, WoO 59 (*Piano Repertoire 7*)
Sonata in G Major, op. 49, no. 2/I (*Piano Repertoire 8*)
Six Easy Variations on an Original Theme, WoO 77 (*Piano Repertoire 9*)
Rondo in C Major, op. 51, no. 1 (*Piano Repertoire 9*)
Sonata in E Major, op. 14, no. 1 (complete) (*Piano Repertoire 10*)

WEB QUEST

There are hundreds of websites devoted to Haydn, Mozart, and Beethoven. Conduct an internet search on at least one of these composers and make a list of your favorite sites. Look for biographical insights, pictures, details about your favorite compositions, and sound clips.

Supplemental Activity: *Mozart and Beethoven at the Movies*

As you complete your study of this unit on the Classical era, you may enjoy watching the award-winning films, *Amadeus* and *Immortal Beloved.* (Caution: Be sure you can distinguish fact from fiction!)

As you watch these movies, listen carefully to the soundtracks. Do you recognize any of the pieces you studied in this unit? With the help of your teacher, identify additional works by Mozart and Beethoven used in the films. Why do you suppose the filmmakers chose those particular pieces?

Film title ______________________________

Composition heard in soundtrack ______________________________

Scene/Plot ______________________________

____

____

____

Film title ______________________________

Composition heard in soundtrack ______________________________

Scene/Plot ______________________________

____

____

____

Film title ______________________________

Composition heard in soundtrack ______________________________

Scene/Plot ______________________________

____

____

____

Review and Reflection

Compare the musical careers of Haydn, Mozart, and Beethoven by completing the chart below:

	Haydn	Mozart	Beethoven
Dates	___	___	___
Birthplace	___	___	___
Education	___ ___	___ ___	___ ___
Instruments played	___ ___	___ ___	___ ___
Travels	___ ___	___ ___	___ ___
Places of employment and/or patrons	___ ___ ___ ___	___ ___ ___ ___	___ ___ ___ ___
Genres cultivated	___ ___ ___ ___ ___	___ ___ ___ ___ ___	___ ___ ___ ___ ___
Hallmarks of individual style	___ ___ ___ ___ ___	___ ___ ___ ___ ___	___ ___ ___ ___ ___

What do *you* like about the music of the Classical period? Do you have a favorite composer or piece? Of the works you studied in this unit, which did you enjoy the most, and why?

____

____

____

____

Quiz

Match each item on the left to one of the descriptions on the right:

________	Esterházy	a. Beethoven's patron
________	Friedrich Schiller	b. Mozart's librettist
________	Archbishop von Colloredo	c. collaborated with Mozart on *The Magic Flute*
________	Bonn	d. Haydn's patron
________	Lorenzo da Ponte	e. Beethoven's birthplace
________	Rohrau	f. wrote Ode to Joy
________	Ludwig Köchel	g. Mozart's patron
________	Salzburg	h. Mozart's birthplace
________	Count Razumowsky	i. Haydn's birthplace
________	Emanuel Schikaneder	j. catalogued Mozart's works

Name each of the following:

A chamber work by Haydn subtitled "The Emperor." ________________

The subtitle of Mozart's *Symphony No. 41.* ________________

The form described as ABACA. ________________

Beethoven's only opera. ________________

The Mozart work completed by Süssmayr. ________________

The chamber ensemble consisting of two violins, viola, and cello. ________________

Mozart's last opera. ________________

The city in which St. Stephen's Cathedral is located. ________________

The key in which *Symphony No. 5*, op. 67 ends. ________________

The individual to whom Beethoven originally dedicated the *Eroica Symphony*. ________________

UNIT FOUR

THE ROMANTIC PERIOD (*ca* 1825–*ca* 1900)

In the surging power of Beethoven's Fifth Symphony, you likely observed a heightened emotionalism and deeply personal expression—characteristics of Romanticism. Beethoven stands as a titan, straddling the Classical and Romantic periods. With these two style periods, it is difficult to pinpoint a specific year to symbolize the twilight of one era and the dawning of a new one: the roots of Romanticism can be traced as far back as the 1770s, particularly in the literary movement known as *Sturm und Drang* (storm and stress).

Before we embark on our exploration of Romantic music, you should have an overview of the cultural and historical events of the time. Examine the timeline below to see how many people and events you recognize. In the space provided, add four additional events or people of interest to you from this era.

Timeline

1825–1900	
Historical Events	• **1830** First railroad (Liverpool–Manchester) • **1837** Coronation of Queen Victoria • **1848** Revolutions throughout Europe • **1859** Darwin's *Origin of Species* • **1865** Abolition of Slavery • **1867** Canada's Confederation • **1869** First exhibit of Impressionist paintings • **1886** Statue of Liberty unveiled
Important Figures	**A. Dudevant** 1804–1876 **F. Nietzsche** 1844–1900 **C. Monet** 1840–1926 **V. van Gogh** 1853–1891 **G.B. Shaw** 1856–1950 **S. Diaghilev** 1872–1929
Composers	**Franz Schubert** 1797–1828 **Hector Berlioz** 1803–1869 **Felix Mendelssohn** 1809–1847 **Robert Schumann** 1810–1856 **Frédéric Chopin** 1810–1849 **Franz Liszt** 1811–1886 **Richard Wagner** 1813–1883 **Giuseppe Verdi** 1813–1901 **Johannes Brahms** 1833–1897 **Georges Bizet** 1838–1875 **Piotr Ilyich Tchaikovsky** 1840–1893 **Giacomo Puccini** 1858–1924
Additional Events/People	

Historical and Cultural Background

Define the term *romanticism*:

____

____

____

____

Which of the following traits and conditions characterize the spirit of the Romantic era?

- ☐ Revived interest in Classical antiquity
- ☐ Uninhibited emotional expression
- ☐ Intensely subjective view of the world
- ☐ Emphasis on form and structure
- ☐ Awareness of nature, often viewed metaphorically
- ☐ Arts rely exclusively on the patronage of the nobility
- ☐ Emergence of the "bohemian" artist
- ☐ Increased use of folk songs and dances
- ☐ Keen interest in the supernatural
- ☐ Age of Absolute Monarchy
- ☐ "Sehnsucht," the yearning for the impossible ideal
- ☐ Revived interest in Gothic culture
- ☐ Morbid fascination with death
- ☐ "Weltschmerz," world-weariness and pessimism

Name some of the historical events and cultural figures that shaped this era:

Historical events 1. ______________________

2. ______________________

3. ______________________

Prominent writers 1. ______________________

2. ______________________

3. ______________________

Painters 1. ____________________

2. ____________________

3. ____________________

What was the French Revolution, and what effect did it have on music?

What was the Industrial Revolution, and what effect did it have on music?

Describe the improvements made to each of the following instruments in the 19th century:

piano ____________________

harp ____________________

brass instruments ____________________

What is a virtuoso?

What position did the virtuoso performer enjoy in 19th-century society?

For each of the following disciplines, name a celebrated Romantic-era virtuoso:

piano ______

violin ______

opera ______

conducting ______

Building a Musical Vocabulary: *Elements of Romantic Style*

Define the following terms as they apply to Romantic music:

program music ______

program symphony ______

symphonic poem/tone poem ______

concert overture ______

nationalism ______

exoticism ______

chromatic harmony ______

bel canto style ______

UNIT FOUR

In terms of their approach to formal structure, how did 19th-century composers differ from their 18th-century counterparts?

____

____

____

____

Listening for Elements of Romantic Style

Part One: Listen to a recording of the well-known *1812 Overture* by Tchaikovsky. From the list below, identify the musical features that are present in this composition:

- ☐ nationalism
- ☐ exoticism
- ☐ virtuosity
- ☐ chromatic harmony
- ☐ sonata form
- ☐ opportunities for use of *rubato*
- ☐ free approach to form
- ☐ exploitation of technological advances to the instrument
- ☐ influence of folk music
- ☐ programmatic elements
- ☐ highly expressive and emotional
- ☐ wide range of dynamics
- ☐ unique instrumentation and special effects

Part Two: From your own repertoire, identify one work from the Romantic era. Refer to the list above and identify the musical features that apply to your piece.

Title ____

Composer ____

Instrument ____

Musical features ____

____

____

____

____

____

____

Schubert and the German Art Song

The Life and Music of Franz Schubert (1797–1828)

Perhaps more than any other 19th-century composer, Schubert lived the life of the so-called "bohemian artist." As a young man, he consciously rejected a secure middle-class existence in order to pursue his art. Unfortunately, Schubert's life was short and marked with financial struggles and poor health.

While Schubert is best known for his contributions to the German art song, or *Lied*, he also composed significant works in virtually all genres. His music represents the confluence of two styles: Classicism, as demonstrated by his approach to form, and Romanticism, as seen in the wide range of emotion found in his music.

Explain Schubert's connection to the following people and places:

Vienna ______________________________

____

____

Franz Theodor Schubert ______________________________

____

____

Imperial Chapel ______________________________

____

____

Antonio Salieri ______________________________

____

____

Johann Wolfgang von Goethe ______________________________

____

____

Wilhelm Müller ______________________________

____

____

Johann Vogl ______________________________

____

____

Beethoven

What was a "Schubertiad"?

In what ways did Schubert's life typify the struggle of the Romantic artist?

For each of the following genres, list Schubert's contributions and innovations:

symphony

chamber music

piano music

songs (Lieder)

song cycles

What does the "D" after titles of Schubert's works signify?

Summarize Schubert's style by listing Classical and Romantic characteristics in his music:

Classical Elements	Romantic Elements
use of sonata form	intensely personal

Building a Musical Vocabulary: *German Art Song*

Define each of the following terms:

art song

folk song

Lied

strophic

modified strophic

durchkomponiert (through-composed) ______________________________

____

____

song cycle ____

____

____

ballad ____

____

____

UNIT FOUR

Required Listening: *Selected Schubert Songs*

The Lied represents the perfect union of poetry and music, singer, and pianist. In Schubert's vast output of Lieder—over 600 have survived—the piano and voice share the responsibility for bringing the poetic images to life.

Choose **ONE** of the following songs by Schubert and listen to a recording. If possible, follow a score while you listen. Complete the required listening outline for the song you have chosen.

Erlkönig, op. 1, D 328
Gretchen am Spinnrade, op. 2, D 118
Die Forelle, op. 32, D 550

Title ____________________ English translation ____________________

Poet ____

Date of composition ____

Song type/structure (choose one):

☐ strophic
☐ modified strophic
☐ *durchkomponiert* (through-composed)

Key ____________________ Meter ____________________

Tempo ____________________

Summarize the content/story of the poem.

____

____

____

____

____

____

What Romantic characteristics are reflected in the poem?

____

____

____

____

Describe how the content of the poem is reflected in each of the following musical aspects:

atmosphere and character ______________________________________

____

____

vocal melody ____

____

____

harmonic language ____

____

____

piano accompaniment ____

____

____

structural design ____

____

____

DID YOU KNOW? It was through the piano transcriptions of Franz Liszt that many of Schubert's compositions were brought to the attention of a wide audience. You may enjoy listening to recordings of some of these transcriptions, noting how skilfully Liszt merges the voice and piano parts to create virtuosic piano solos. All three of the required listening choices were transcribed.

Recommended Listening for Schubert:
Piano Quintet in A Major, op. 114, D 667 ("Trout")
Symphony No. 8 in B Minor, D 759 ("Unfinished")
Impromptu in E flat Major, op. 90, no. 2, D 899
String Quartet No. 14 in D Minor, D 810 ("Death and the Maiden")
Ave Maria, op. 52, no. 6, D 839

Schubert Works in *Celebration Series Perspectives®*:
Impromptu, op. 142, no. 2 (*Piano Repertoire 9*)

Chopin and Romantic Piano Music

The Life and Music of Frédéric Chopin (1810–1849)

Unlike any composer of his time, Chopin chose to concentrate almost exclusively on piano music. A national hero in his native Poland, Chopin is universally acclaimed as the "poet of the piano." His lyricism and progressive harmony opened new worlds of pianistic color, and his use of unique and innovative textures and figurations places him alongside his contemporary Franz Liszt in terms of significance. Chopin and Liszt, each in his own way, raised the level of piano virtuosity to unprecedented heights.

Explain Chopin's connection to the following people and places:

Żelazowa Wola ______________________________

____

Nicolas and Justyna Chopin ______________________________

Warsaw ______________________________

____

Konstancja Gladkowska ______________________________

Jozef Elsner ______________________________

____

____

Vienna

Robert Schumann

Paris

Franz Liszt

George Sand

Majorca

Jane Stirling

Père Lachaise Cemetery

What hardships did Chopin endure during his lifetime?

How did Chopin's primary focus as a composer differ from that of his contemporaries?

Which aspects of Chopin's pianism earned him the respect of his peers?

Comment on Chopin's attitude toward public and private performance.

What were Chopin's feelings about opera, and how are they reflected in his compositional style?

How was Chopin's Polish heritage expressed in his music?

Building a Musical Vocabulary: *Romantic Piano Music*

Define the following terms:

character piece

polonaise

rubato

ternary form ____________________

____

____

mazurka ____________________

____

____

waltz ____________________

____

____

étude ____________________

____

____

nocturne ____________________

____

____

UNIT FOUR

Required Listening: *Selected Piano Works*

Choose **EITHER** *Polonaise in A flat Major*, op. 53, **OR** *Nocturne in C Minor*, op. 48, no. 1. Listen to a recording. If possible, follow a score while you listen. Complete the listening outline for the piece you have chosen.

Polonaise in A flat Major, op. 53

In 1830, at the age of twenty, Chopin departed from his native Poland, eager to explore professional opportunities abroad. Although he never returned to his homeland, he kept his patriotism alive through nationalistic piano pieces such as *mazurkas* and *polonaises.*

Year of composition __________ Genre __________

Principal key __________ Meter __________

Form __________

Introduction

Ex. 4.1 Chopin, *Polonaise in A flat Major*, op. 53, mm. 1-4.

By what musical means does Chopin generate tension in the opening measures of this piece?

____

____

Section A

Ex. 4.2 Chopin, *Polonaise in A flat Major*, op. 53, mm. 17-20.

Describe what each hand plays in the opening of Section A (Ex. 4.2), commenting on rhythmic, harmonic, and pianistic elements:

RH ____

LH ____

The music in Section A is punctuated on several occasions with a brilliant ascending scale passage. How many times does this passage occur? __________

Within Section A, there is a contrasting middle section consisting of two subsidiary themes (mm. 49-56 and mm. 57-64). Comment on how the Polonaise character is preserved here.

Section B

Ex. 4.3 Chopin, *Polonaise in A flat Major*, op. 53, mm. 85-88.

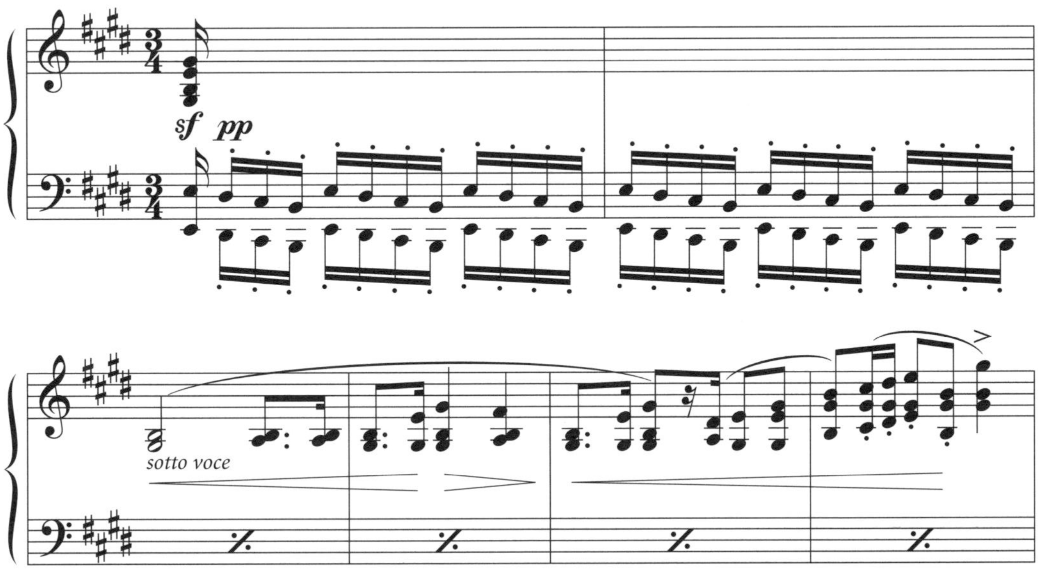

What is the new key at the beginning of this section? __________________

Although at face value this may seem only remotely related to the home key, it is actually an enharmonic respelling of F flat major (the flattened sixth). Why did Chopin make this adjustment?

How does Chopin achieve a proud martial character in this passage?

After two statements of the E major theme accompanied by octaves, there is a dramatic shift down a half-step to the key of D sharp major (mm. 116-119). Explain the relationship of this key to the home key.

This dramatic transition leads to another subsidiary theme at m. 121. What new character or mood is established here?

Return of Section A (m. 155)
Compare this to the opening section. How has it been altered?

Coda (m. 171)
From what materials is this section derived, and how does it provide a dramatic conclusion to the piece?

With your teacher's help, use the space below to draw a simple structural diagram of this piece, showing major sections, keys, and contrasting thematic material or sub-sections.

How did Chopin express his national heritage in this composition?

List four specific technical challenges a pianist will encounter in this virtuosic work:

1. ____

____

2. ____

____

3. ____

____

4. ____

____

Nocturne in C Minor, op. 48, no. 1

While the nocturnes of John Field (1782–1837) may have been a point of departure, it was Chopin's ingenuity that elevated the nocturne to an eloquent, sophisticated form. The *Nocturne in C Minor* was written in the final decade of his life and is considered one of his mature works. Chopin wrote twenty-one nocturnes, and although this majestic piece is part of the same family of works, in several respects it is unlike many of the others. When you complete your study of this piece, you may enjoy comparing it to one or more additional nocturnes by Chopin.

Key ____________________ Tempo ______________________________

Meter __________________ Approximate date of composition __________

The formal structure of this work can be designated as **A B A¹**

A	**B**	**A¹**
mm. 1-24	mm. 25-48	mm. 49-77

What term describes this form? __________________

Section A

Ex. 4.4 Chopin, *Nocturne in C Minor*, op. 48, no. 1, mm. 1-4.

Describe the left-hand accompaniment found in the opening of Section A (Ex. 4.4).

____

____

Which of the following best describes the character of the opening section?

a) delicate and gentle

b) agitated and passionate

c) noble and stately

The opening melody occurs two more times after the first statement, with a different harmonic underpinning each time:

Ex. 4.5 Chopin, *Nocturne in C Minor*, op. 48, no. 1, mm. 5 and 6.

Ex. 4.6 Chopin, *Nocturne in C Minor*, op. 48, no. 1, mm. 17 and 18.

Analyze the harmonic progression in the three statements shown in Ex. 4.4, 4.5, and 4.6. What is the effect of these variants?

____

____

____

At m. 9, there is an unexpected modulation:

Ex. 4.7 Chopin, *Nocturne in C Minor*, op. 48, no. 1, mm. 9 and 10.

Which of the following is the new key in Ex. 4.7?

a) D flat major
b) E flat major
c) C major

How is this new key related to the original tonic of C minor?

a) ♭VI
b) ♭II
c) relative major

This key can also be referred to as the ________________ of C minor.

Describe Chopin's use of melodic decoration in Ex. 4.7 and other similar passages.

____

____

Section B

Ex. 4.8 Chopin, *Nocturne in C Minor*, op. 48, no. 1, mm. 25-28.

Which of the following describes how Section B begins?

a) a march-like theme in chorale style
b) a polyphonic section resembling a fugue
c) a lyrical cantabile right hand with arpeggio accompaniment

What does the indication *poco più lento* suggest? ________________

Is this indication observed in the recording you are listening to? ________________

What does *sotto voce* indicate? ________________

Is this indication observed in the recording you are listening to? ________________

Which of the following interrupts the melody part way into Section B (m. 39)?

a) rumbling octaves in triplet rhythm
b) a return of the opening theme
c) trills in the right hand

These interruptions gradually become longer and more insistent, and continue until the end of Section B. Which of the following describes the resulting change in character?

a) intense and agitated
b) calm and serene
c) playful and mischievous

Section A[1] (m. 40)
At the return of Section A, what does the indication *doppio movimento* suggest?

____

Is this indication observed in the recording you are listening to? ____________

Although the melody line is the same as the opening, how has the music been altered in this section?

a) change of key
b) change of meter
c) change of accompaniment figure

When the triplet pattern from Section B octaves is combined with the opening melody, what is the resulting musical character?

a) agitated and restless
b) serene and calm
c) pensive and thoughtful

The tension continues to build, reaching a climactic point in mm. 69-72. List three ways in which this momentum is achieved in the recording you listened to.

____

____

____

____

____

Describe how the nocturne concludes, and its musical effect.

____

____

What elements of this piece do you find most appealing?

____

Name two composers who wrote nocturnes after Chopin.

______________________ ______________________

Although Chopin was buried at the Père Lachaise Cemetery in Paris, he had requested that his heart be taken back to Poland. His request was honored, and Chopin's heart is now located at the Church of the Holy Cross in Warsaw. Every year, thousands of admirers flock there to pay their respects to this beloved composer.

Recommended Listening for Chopin:
Etude in E Major, op. 10, no. 3
Etude in C Minor, op. 10, no. 12 ("Revolutionary")
Mazurka in A Minor, op. 17, no. 4
Ballade in G Minor, op. 23, no. 1
24 Preludes, op. 28
Piano Concerto in E Minor, op. 11, no. 1
Cello Sonata in G Minor, op. 65

Chopin Works in *Celebration Series Perspectives®*:
Prelude in E Minor, op. 28, no. 4 (*Piano Repertoire 7*)
Prelude in B Minor, op. 28, no. 6 (*Piano Repertoire 8*)
Nocturne in C sharp Minor, op. posth. / KK IVa 16 (*Piano Repertoire 9*)
Waltz in G flat Major, op. posth. 70, no. 1, CT 217 (*Piano Repertoire 9*)
Polonaise in C sharp Minor, op. 26, no. 1 (*Piano Repertoire 10*)
Nocturne in F sharp Major, op. 15, no. 2 (*Piano Repertoire 10*)

Berlioz and *Symphonie fantastique*

The Life and Music of Hector Berlioz (1803–1869)

Hector Berlioz stands apart from his contemporaries in that he was not a virtuoso performer. He himself acknowledged that this left him free to explore the unique capabilities of each instrument in the orchestra. Like many Romantic composers, Berlioz sought to find the connections between music and literature; the writings of Shakespeare, Byron, and Goethe especially fired his imagination. Berlioz documented the details of his colorful life in an autobiography—one of only a handful of composers to have done so. The composer's eccentric personality is best exemplified by his notorious and highly publicized romantic affairs.

Explain Berlioz's connection to the following people and places:

Côte-Saint-André ______________________________

Louis Berlioz ______________________________

Paris ______________________________

____

____

Paris Conservatoire ______________________________

____

Harriet Smithson ______________________________

____

____

Franz Liszt ______________________________

____

Marie ("Camille") Moke ______________________________

____

Rome ______________________________

____

F.A. Habeneck ______________________________

Marie Recio ______________________________

What special honors were bestowed upon Berlioz:

by the Paris Conservatoire in 1830? ______________________________

by the French government later in his life? ______________________________

Explain how the work of the following artists had an impact on Berlioz:

Shakespeare ______________________________

____

____

Byron ______________________________

____

____

Goethe ____

____

____

Beethoven ____

____

____

In addition to being a talented composer, conductor, and music critic, Berlioz was also the author of several important literary works. Explain the significance of the following:

Grand traité d'instrumentation ____

____

____

Mémoires de Hector Berlioz ____

____

____

____

For each of the following genres, list Berlioz's contributions and innovations:

concert overture ____

____

____

choral music ____

____

opera ____

____

art song ____

____

program symphony ____

____

____

UNIT FOUR

Required Listening: *Symphonie fantastique*

This spellbinding composition, sprung entirely from Berlioz's fertile imagination, illustrates the Romantic fascination with the supernatural and the bizarre. Even today, audiences are mesmerized by the highly unique orchestration and the way it mirrors the macabre plot. After you listen to *Symphonie fantastique*, try to imagine the impact it made on the audience of Berlioz's day!

Berlioz's *Symphonie fantastique* is a Romantic *program symphony*. This new genre evolved when 19th-century composers merged the structure of the Classical symphony with the descriptive nature of program music. Beethoven actually opened the door to this creative development with his sixth symphony, the "Pastoral," which depicted various aspects of nature. (The five-movement construction and descriptive titles of that work were unprecedented in the Classical era.)

Listen to a recording of *Symphonie fantastique*. If possible, follow a score while you listen. Answer the following general questions about this symphony, then construct an overview of the first four movements by completing the outlines provided. Complete the detailed outline for the fifth movement.

UNIT FOUR

What is the full title of this work? ______________________________

Date of composition __________

What was Berlioz trying to suggest with this title?

____

____

Summarize briefly the general program of this work.

____

____

____

____

____

Berlioz used a large orchestra for this symphony and wrote very specific performance indications. Explain the following:

ophicléide ______________________________

____

portamento ______________________________

____

col legno ____

____

cloches ____

____

Explain the term *idée fixe.* ______________________________

Whom does the *idée fixe* represent in this work? ______________

In which movements is this theme heard? ____________________

First Movement

Title: ______________________

Ex. 4.9 Berlioz, *Symphonie fantastique*/I, *idée fixe.*

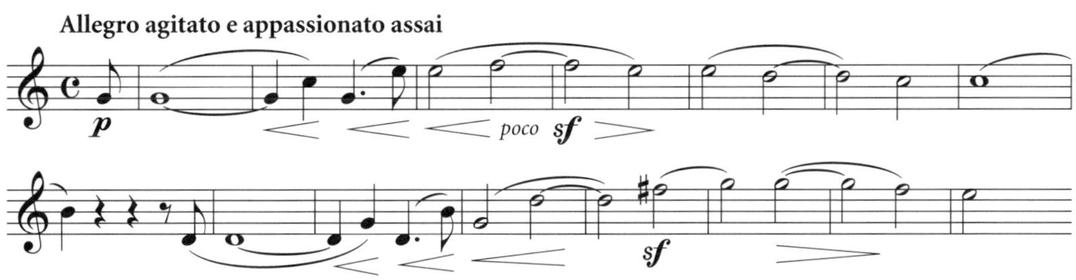

Key: opens in _____ minor but with the appearance of the *idée fixe* shifts to _____ major.

Tempo: opens ________________; later becomes ________________

Program ____

____

____

____

Second Movement

Title ______________________________________

Key ________________ Tempo ________________

Meter ________________ Dance type represented ________________

Program ___

___

___

___

What instrument is featured in the opening measures? ___

Third Movement

Title ___

Key ___ Tempo ___

Meter ___

Program ___

___

___

___

Which instrument opens this movement? ___

Which instrument answers? ___ What special direction does Berlioz give to this performer? (Hint: Where is he/she positioned?)

___

What effect does this create? ___

___

Fourth Movement

Title ___

Key ___ Tempo ___

Meter ___

Program ___

___

___

___

At the end of the movement, which instrument starts to play the *idée fixe* but gets interrupted? ___

What grisly picture is depicted at this point, and how did Berlioz achieve his desired effect?

____

____

Fifth Movement

Title ____________________

Key: opens in ____________________

Tempo: opens in ____________________; later changes to ____________________

Meter ____________________

Program ____

____

____

____

What is the general mood of the introduction? How does Berlioz achieve such spectral sounds?

____

____

____

Which instrument plays the *idée fixe* when the Allegro section begins? __________

Ex. 4.10 Berlioz, *Symphonie fantastique*/V, *idée fixe*.

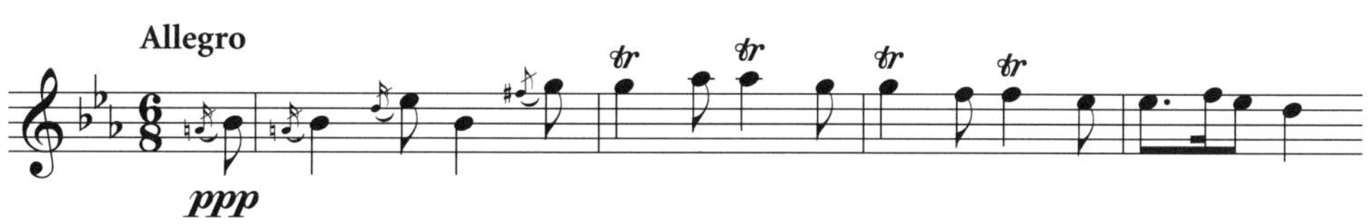

What new key is established in Ex. 4.10? __________

What has happened to "the beloved" in this section? By what musical means does Berlioz achieve such a *macabre* effect?

____

____

The upcoming "Dance of the Witches" is briefly foreshadowed, then followed by the ominous chiming of bells on the tonic and dominant notes.

Next the grim-sounding *Dies irae* is played:

Ex. 4.11 Berlioz, *Symphonie fantastique*/V, *Dies irae.*

What does *Dies irae* mean in English? ______________________________

What is the origin of this familiar theme, and why is it so appropriate to the story line of this movement?

____

____

____

____

Describe Berlioz's treatment of the *Dies irae* theme in terms of orchestration, rhythm, and texture.

____

____

____

____

What unusual 19th-century instrument (now replaced with tubas) did the score originally require here? ______________________________

The passage based on the *Dies irae* leads into the "Dance of the Witches" section:

Ex. 4.12 Berlioz, *Symphonie fantastique*/V, "Dance of the Witches."

What is the new key in Ex. 4.12? ________________
(This key will prevail for the remainder of the movement.)

What is the principal texture of this passage? ________________

What musical elements contribute to the mocking tone?

____

____

____

____

In the closing section of this movement, Berlioz combines two themes heard earlier. What are they? ____________________ and ____________________

What makes the climax of this work so memorable?

List five specific characteristics of Romanticism exemplified in *Symphonie fantastique:*

1. ____________________

2. ____________________

3. ____________________

4. ____________________

5. ____________________

DID YOU KNOW?

In 1832, Berlioz created a sequel to *Symphonie fantastique* entitled "*Lélio, ou Le Retour à la vie, monodrame lyrique.*" In this unique work, scored for orchestra, chorus, and narrator, the story line of *Symphonie fantastique* is continued. Lélio, the lovesick protagonist we came to know in *Symphonie fantastique*, now finds a certain tranquility, largely through the redemptive powers of music and art.

Recommended Listening for Berlioz:
Les nuits d'été, op. 7
Romeo and Juliet Symphony, op. 17
Harold in Italy, op. 16
Lélio, op. 14b
L'Enfance du Christ, op. 25

Bizet and *Carmen*

The Life and Music of Georges Bizet (1838–1875)

While Georges Bizet's precocious talent as a student garnered him the "Prix de Rome," his fame rests on his exotic and passionate opera *Carmen.* The fascinating characters, engaging arias, orchestral color, and rhythmic vitality all contribute to this work's enduring popularity. Sadly, Bizet did not live long enough to enjoy *Carmen*'s acclaim and international success.

Explain Bizet's connection to the following people and places:

Paris ______________________________

____

Paris Conservatoire ______________________________

____

Charles Gounod ______________________________

____

L'Opéra-Comique ______________________________

____

Leon Carvalho ______________________________

____

Rome ______________________________

____

Ernest Guiraud ______________________________

____

Geneviève Halèvy ______________________________

____

Meilhac & Halèvy ______________________________

____

Translate these titles and identify the genre of the following important works by Bizet:

	Translation	Genre
L'Arlésienne	____________	____________
Les pêcheurs de perles	____________	____________
Djamileh	____________	____________
Jeux d'enfants	____________	____________
La jolie fille de Perth	____________	____________

Building a Musical Vocabulary: *Opera*

Explain the following terms:

opera ____

____

____

grand opera ____

____

____

opéra-comique ____

____

____

lyric opera ____

____

____

overture ____

____

____

prelude ____

____

____

UNIT FOUR

libretto ____

____

____

recitative ____

____

____

aria ____

____

____

Name one opera by each of these leading 19th-century composers:

Rossini ______________________ Bellini ______________________

Donizetti ______________________ Verdi ______________________

Puccini ______________________ Wagner ______________________

WEB QUEST

Opera lovers can access a wealth of information on the internet. There are plot summaries, libretto translations, behind the scenes information, discussion groups, and much more. Learn more about opera by visiting the official site of a major opera house like the Metropolitan Opera, the San Francisco Opera, the Canadian Opera Company, or simply search on words and phrases like *opera*, *opera singers*, and *opera history*.

The Plot and Characters of *Carmen*

In what city and year did *Carmen* receive its premiere? ______________________

Who wrote the original novella that inspired this work? ______________________

Name the two individuals who wrote the libretto:

______________________ and ______________________

In which language was the opera written? ______________________

Provide a brief explanation for the following Spanish and exotic elements in *Carmen*:

habañera ____

____

seguidilla ______________________________

____

gypsy ______________________________

____

toreador ______________________________

____

flamenco ______________________________

____

Describe the principal characters in *Carmen* and identify their voice types where indicated:

Carmen (mezzo-soprano) ______________________________

____

____

Don José (______________) ______________________________

Micaela (______________) ______________________________

Escamillo (______________) ______________________________

Lt. Zuniga ______________________________

Mercedes and Frasquita ______________________________

Summarize the events that unfold in each act:

Act One

Setting Seville (Spain); a city square outside the cigarette factory

____

____

____

____

____

____

____

Act Two

Setting

Act Three

Setting

Act Four

Setting

DID YOU KNOW?

The original version of *Carmen*—the one most frequently performed today—contains much spoken dialogue. However, shortly after Bizet's death, Ernest Guiraud, a friend and colleague of the composer, set the spoken parts to *recitative*. The Imperial State Opera had requested this revision for its Vienna premiere in 1875.

Required Listening: Selections from *Carmen*

Listen to a recording of *Carmen*, or watch a videotaped performance. If possible, follow a score while you listen. Complete the listening outlines for **BOTH** the *Prelude* and *Habañera* from Act One.

Act One, Prelude

The form of this composition is A – B – A – C.

Section A

Ex. 4.13 Bizet, *Carmen*, Prelude to Act One, main theme.

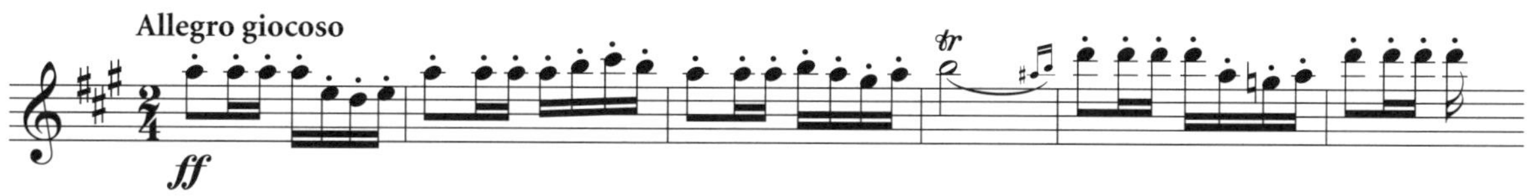

Key ______________________ Tempo ______________________

Meter ______________________

By what musical means does Bizet achieve such a sunny, festive sound?

____

____

Section B

Ex. 4.14 Bizet, *Carmen*, Prelude to Act One, toreador theme.

New key ______________________ (Hint: Look at the accidentals!)

Describe this theme and the orchestration.

____

____

____

____

____

(Section A returns, abbreviated.)

Section C
The famous "Fate" motive is introduced:

Ex. 4.15 Bizet, *Carmen*, Prelude to Act One, Fate motive.

How does Bizet create a dark and foreboding atmosphere here?

____

____

____

Cite three places (scenes) in the opera where this important motive recurs:

1. ____

2. ____

3. ____

Act One, *Habañera*

Which character sings this aria? ____________________

Recitative: "Quand je vous aimerai...c'est certain..."
Carmen is responding to the attention of the young men in the square. What does she tell them?

____

____

What thematic material does Bizet interject between the words "peut-être demain" and "n'est pas aujourd'hui"? How has it been altered?

____

____

____

Aria (with Chorus): "L'amour est un oiseau rebelle..."

Ex. 4.16 Bizet, *Carmen*, Act One, "L'amour est un oiseau rebelle...".

Key ______________________ Tempo ______________________

Meter ______________________

Carmen's true nature is revealed directly and honestly in this aria. What is she expressing?

____

____

____

Describe the music in the aria by commenting on the following elements:

melody ____

____

harmony ____

____

rhythm ____

____

use of chorus ____

____

orchestration ____

____

Immediately after Carmen sings this aria, she confronts Don José and throws something at him. What does she toss? ____________________

What music accompanies this action and what does it signify?

If you were directing *Carmen*, what qualities of the heroine's character would you try to bring out?

DID YOU KNOW?

The melody of the habañera in *Carmen* was not actually composed by Bizet. Having heard this tune earlier, and under the mistaken impression that it was a folksong, Bizet incorporated it into his opera. Only later did he learn that the original song, entitled *El arreglits* ("A Little Arrangement"), was composed by Sebastien de Yradier.

Recommended Listening for Bizet:
Symphony in C
"Au fond du temple saint" (duet from *Les pêcheurs de perles*)
Carmen Fantasy by Pablo Sarasate

Supplemental Activity: *Comparing Recordings of Carmen*

The role of Carmen was intended for a mezzo-soprano but that hasn't stopped sopranos from singing the part. Listen to two recordings, one in which Carmen is sung by a mezzo-soprano, the other by a soprano. Write your impressions in the space provided.

Mezzo-Soprano ____________________ (Singer's name)

Soprano ____________________ (Singer's name)

Puccini and *Madama Butterfly*

The Life and Music of Giacomo Puccini (1858–1924)

Giacomo Puccini began his career in the shadow of Giuseppe Verdi (1813–1901). That he was able to forge a wholly new style is as much a testament to his genius as to his canny ability to gauge the public's taste. Puccini tapped into audiences' fascination with melodrama, fast-paced action, and devastating emotional entanglements to create, together with some of his contemporaries, the *verismo* movement.

Puccini's sweeping melodic curves and poignant harmonies are greatly admired, but if any one aspect of his work stands out, it is the vivid musical portraits of his operatic heroines. These women stay with us long after the curtain has fallen. With Mimi, the consumptive seamstress from *La bohème,* Tosca, the diva from the opera with the same name, or Cio-Cio-San, the young geisha from *Madama Butterfly*, Puccini suggests both fragility and strength.

Explain Puccini's connection to the following people and places:

Lucca ______________________________

Milan Conservatory ______________________________

____

Giulio Ricordi ______________________________

____

Elvira Gemignani ______________________________

David Belasco ______________________________

____

Metropolitan Opera ______________________________

____

Arturo Toscanini ______________________________

____

Three famous Puccini operas (*La bohème, Tosca, Madama Butterfly*) have already been mentioned. Name four additional operas by Puccini:

______________ ______________

______________ ______________

The terms and musical elements below are related to Puccini's operas. Provide an explanation of each:

exoticism ______________________________

____

____

verismo ______________________________

____

____

pentatonic scale ______________________________

____

____

whole-tone scale ______________________________

____

____

UNIT FOUR

The Plot and Characters of *Madama Butterfly*

Who wrote the original novella that inspired this work? ______________________

In which language was the opera written? ______________________

Opera type ______________________________

In what city and year did *Madama Butterfly* receive its premiere?

______________________ ____________

Name the two individuals who wrote the libretto.

______________________ and ______________________

On what was the libretto based? ______________________________

Describe the principal characters in this opera and identify their voice types where indicated:

"Butterfly" – Cio-Cio-San (soprano) ______________________________

____

Suzuki (______________________) ______________________________

____

B.F. Pinkerton (____________________) ____

Sharpless (____________________) ____

Additional Characters: Kate Pinkerton (American wife), Goro (a marriage broker), Prince Yamadori, The Bonze (Cio-Cio-San's uncle), Trouble (Cio-Cio-San's child).

Setting: A house on a hilltop in Nagasaki, Japan.

Summarize the events that unfold in each act:

Act One ____

Act Two ____

Act Three ____

Required Listening: Selections from *Madama Butterfly*

Listen to a recording of *Madama Butterfly*, or watch a videotaped performance. If possible, follow a score while you listen. Complete the required listening outlines for **BOTH** the Prelude from Act One and "Un bel di vedremo" from Act Two.

Act One, Prelude

Ex. 4.17 Puccini, *Madama Butterfly*, Prelude to Act One, opening theme.

Key ____________________ Tempo ____________________

Meter ____________________ Texture ____________________

Which orchestral family is featured in this opening section? ____________________

What Baroque form is suggested in these first thirty measures? ____________________

The opening subject is marked *vigoroso.* How does Puccini capture this agitated quality?

____

____

____

____

____

The contrapuntal opening of this opera is clearly rooted in the European tradition. In contrast, the final moments of the opera feature a monophonic melody intoned by unison orchestra, evoking a Japanese style. By framing the opera in this way, Puccini suggested the marked differences between East and West and created a musical backdrop for the tragic consequences that can result when two worlds collide.

Act Two, "Un bel di vedremo"

Character singing ____________________ Voice type ____________________

To whom is she singing? ____________________

What sad prediction does Suzuki make that causes Butterfly to sing this fervent aria?

____

____

____

In this aria Cio-Cio-San expresses her *credo,* her reason for living. What is she telling Suzuki?

____

____

____

The aria may be loosely regarded as having the following form: A-B-A^1-C

Section A

Ex. 4.18 Puccini, *Madama Butterfly*, Act Two, "Un bel di vedremo" (opening).

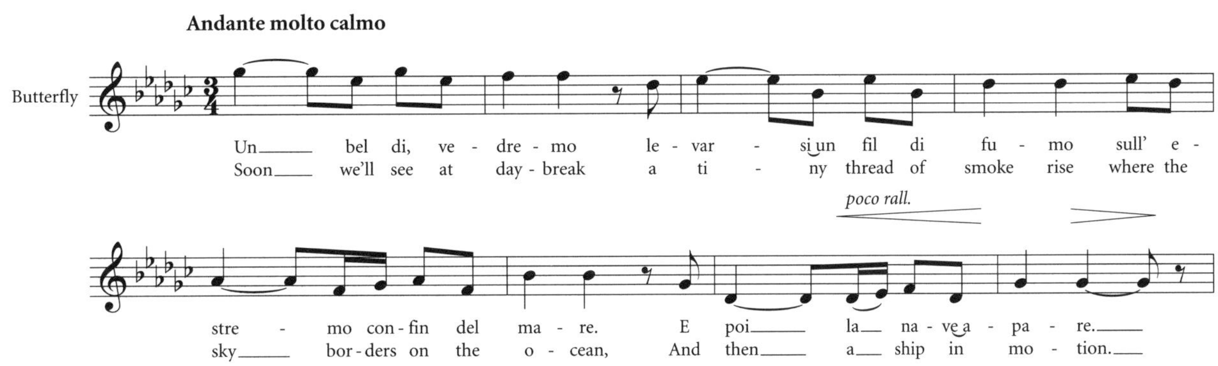

Key ____________________ Tempo ____________________

Meter ____________________ Texture ____________________

Describe the melodic contour of the aria's opening, shown in Ex. 4.18.

____

Describe the orchestral accompaniment and its relationship to the vocal line.

____

Section B

Ex. 4.19 Puccini, *Madama Butterfly*, Act Two, "Un bel di vedremo" (Section B).

In Section B, at "Mi metto là sul ciglio del colle," Puccini adopts a more recitative-like style. By what musical means does he achieve this?

____

____

____

Section A[1]

Ex. 4.20 Puccini, *Madama Butterfly*, Act Two, "Un bel di vedremo" (return of opening theme).

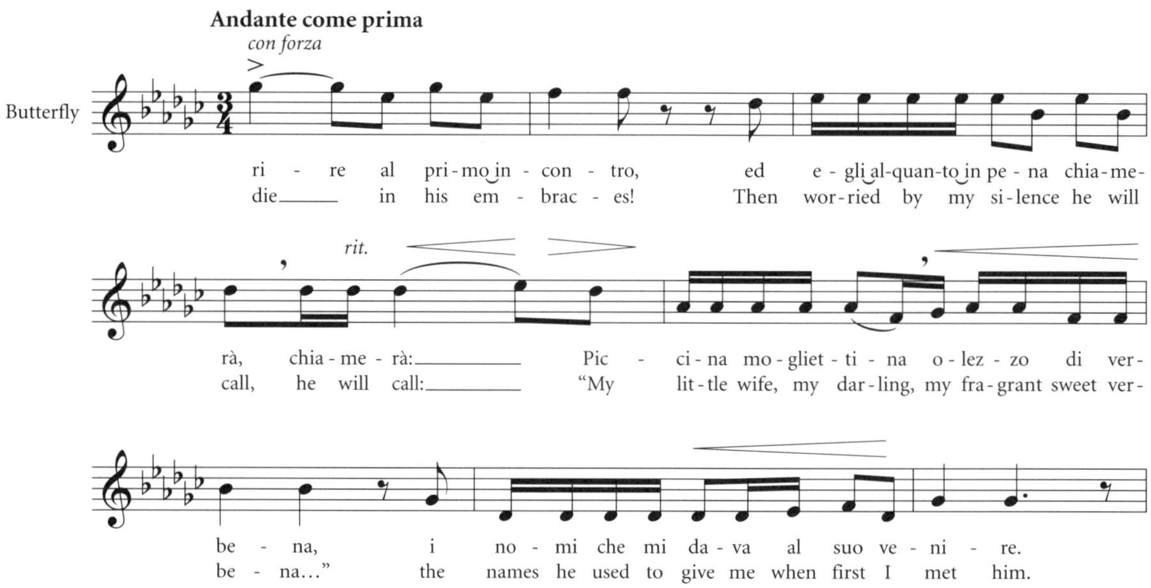

A climactic moment occurs within the return of Section A. On what word does the melody's opening high G flat occur? ______________________

What does this mean in English? ______________________

How does this climax foreshadow later events?

____

____

____

Section C

Ex. 4.21 Puccini, *Madama Butterfly,* Act Two, "Un bel di vedremo" (Section C).

With Section C, at "Tutto questo avverra," Puccini again returns to a recitative-like style. By what musical means does he suggest Butterfly's unwavering faith?

____

____

____

What material forms the basis for the orchestral postlude that concludes the aria?

____

In the works of Chopin that you studied earlier, you came to understand the importance of *rubato* in the performance of his music. How does Puccini create a sense of *rubato* in this aria?

____

____

The story of *Madama Butterfly* inspired the hit musical *Miss Saigon,* which premiered in London in 1989 and started on Broadway in 1991. The creators, Alain Boublil and Claude-Michel Schonberg (the same team behind *Les Misérables*), moved the action from turn-of-the-century Nagasaki to Vietnam during the 1970s. Even in *Miss Saigon's* rich contemporary score one can find influences and even direct quotes from Puccini.

Recommended Listening for Puccini:
Madama Butterfly (Duet: "Vogliatemi bene," Aria: "Che tua madre," Aria: "Tu, tu... Piccolo Iddio")
Tosca (Aria: "Vissi d'arte," Aria: "E lucevan le stelle")
Gianni Shicchi (Aria: "Oh! mio babbino caro")
Turandot (Aria: "Nessun dorma," Aria: "In questa reggia")

Supplemental Activity: *Looking at Romantic Art*

As you have already discovered, developments in music often parallel trends and movements in other art forms. This is definitely the case in the Romantic era. Prominent painters from this period include Eugène Delacroix, Caspar David Friedrich, and Francisco Goya. Their works vividly demonstrate Romantic ideals.

For each of the style traits listed below, identify one Romantic painting that demonstrates the same feature. You may wish to look at paintings in your local art gallery, in art books, or search for paintings and museums on the internet.

	Romantic Painting	**Artist**
nationalism	Liberty Leading the People	Delacroix
exoticism		
interest in the supernatural		
morbid fascination with death		
interest in folk elements		
influence of Shakespeare		
nature viewed metaphorically		

UNIT FOUR

Now that you have sampled several compositions from the 19th century, comment on the following features of Romantic style as they relate to specific composers and works:

lyrical melody ______________________________

____

expressive harmony ______________________________

____

dynamic range ______________________________

____

heightened emotionalism ______________________________

____

expanded virtuosity ______________________________

____

musical nationalism ______________________________

____

musical exoticism ______________________________

____

programmatic element ______________________________

____

orchestral color ______________________________

____

formal design ______________________________

____

Review and Reflection

What do *you* like best about Romantic music? Do you have a favorite composer or piece from the 19th century? Of the works you studied in this unit, which did you enjoy the most, and why?

____

____

____

Quiz

1. For each item listed below, name at least one associated composition from the Romantic era:

   idée fixe ______________________________

   exoticism ______________________________

   ternary form ______________________________

   ophicléide ______________________________

   virtuosity ______________________________

   song cycle ______________________________

   Polish nationalism ______________________________

   Dies irae ______________________________

   oratorio ______________________________

   seguidilla ______________________________

2. Explain the difference between the following:

   through-composed and strophic form ______________________________

   ____

   ____

UNIT FOUR

program music and absolute music

nationalism and exoticism

grand opera and *opéra comique*

habañera and polonaise

UNIT FIVE

THE 20th CENTURY

No other century in history has witnessed such rapid technological advancement. Contemporaries of Beethoven could not possibly have imagined that within a mere one hundred years, a flying machine would be invented, and that sixty years later a man would land on the moon! The phonograph, radio, tape recorder, computer, and internet have expanded our awareness of music on a global scale, and have made it more readily available. A myriad of classical and popular music styles have been developed, many embracing new technology and cross-cultural elements.

Before we embark on our exploration of 20th-century music, you should have an overview of the important cultural and historic events from the century. Examine the timeline below to see how many people and events you recognize. In the space provided, add four additional events or people of interest to you.

Timeline

1900 — 2000

Historical Events

- **1889** Paris World Exposition
- **1895** Marconi's wireless telegraph
- **1903** Wright Brothers first successful airplane flight
- **1914** World War I begins
- **1917** Russian Revolution
- **1920** Women's suffrage
- **1939** World War II begins
- **1945** Atomic bomb dropped on Hiroshima
- **1969** American astronauts walk on the moon
- **1973** Cease-fire declared in Vietnam War
- **1991** Soviet Union dissolved

Composers

Claude Debussy 1862–1918	**Béla Bartók** 1881–1945	**Duke Ellington** 1899–1974	**Leonard Bernstein** 1918–1990
Arnold Schoenberg 1874–1951	**Igor Stravinsky** 1882–1971	**Aaron Copland** 1900–1990	**R. Murray Schafer** 1933–
Maurice Ravel 1875–1937	**Sergei Prokofiev** 1891–1953	**Olivier Messiaen** 1908–1992	**Steve Reich** 1936–
			Alexina Louie 1949–

Additional Events/People

Historical and Cultural Background

List five inventions or technological advancements from the 20th century and comment on their impact on music:

1. ______________________________

____

____

2. ______________________________

____

____

3. ______________________________

____

____

4. ______________________________

____

____

5. ______________________________

____

____

Name five individuals who made significant contributions to the following disciplines in the 20th century:

Politics
1. ______________________________
2. ______________________________
3. ______________________________
4. ______________________________
5. ______________________________

Literature
1. ______________________________
2. ______________________________
3. ______________________________
4. ______________________________
5. ______________________________

Visual Arts 1. ______________________________

2. ______________________________

3. ______________________________

4. ______________________________

5. ______________________________

In the art world, Impressionism and Expressionism were two important movements during the late-19th and early-20th centuries. Outline the fundamental principles that characterize these styles, and name two leading figures whose work embodies these traits.

Impressionism ______________________________

____

____

____

____

Artists 1. ______________ 2. ______________

Expressionism ______________________________

____

____

____

____

Artists 1. ______________ 2. ______________

Building a Musical Vocabulary: *Elements of 20th-century Style*

Match each term to the appropriate definition below:

aleatoric	pentatonic scale	tone row
atonality	polychords	twelve-tone music
expanded tonality	polyrhythm	whole-tone scale
modality	polytonality	

______________ A scale comprised entirely of whole-steps.

______ A five-note scale generally associated with non-Western music.

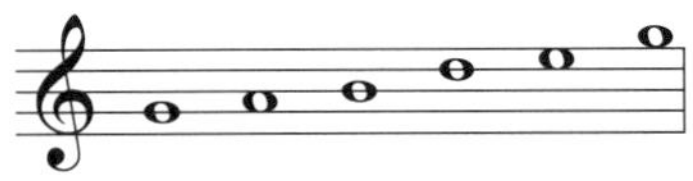

______ The total absence of any tonal center.

______ Two or more tonal centers used simultaneously.

______ Two or more chords combined to form a more complex harmonic unit.

______ Extremely chromatic harmony, still maintaining allegiance to a tonal center.

______ Arrangement of the twelve chromatic pitches within an octave, serving as the basis of a dodecaphonic (twelve-tone) composition.

______ Music based on scales in which the pattern of whole-tones and semi tones is different from conventional major and minor scales (Dorian, Lydian, etc.).

______ Simultaneous use of varying rhythmic or metric patterns.

______ The element of chance, also known as "indeterminacy" (from "alea," meaning dice).

______ Music based on a serial ordering of all twelve chromatic pitches, most commonly associated with composer Arnold Schoenberg.

The musical currents listed below were important in 20th-century music. Elaborate on each trend and name two composers associated with each:

Post-Romanticism ______

______

______

______

Composers 1. ______ 2. ______

Impressionism ______

______

______

______

Composers 1. ______ 2. ______

Expressionism ______________________________

____

____

____

Composers 1. ______________ 2. ______________

serialism ______________________________

____

____

____

Composers 1. ______________ 2. ______________

Neo-Classicism ______________________________

____

____

____

Composers 1. ______________ 2. ______________

non-Western influences ______________________________

____

____

____

Composers 1. ______________ 2. ______________

jazz influence ______________________________

____

____

____

Composers 1. ______________ 2. ______________

use of technology ______________________________

____

____

____

Composers 1. ______________ 2. ______________

minimalism ____

____

____

____

Composers 1. ____________________ 2. ____________________

Listening for Elements of 20th-century Style

Part One: Listen to recordings of three works from the choices identified below. From the list of musical elements that follows, identify the musical features that are present in each work you listened to, and record your personal impressions.

Listening Choices:
Rhapsody in Blue by George Gershwin
Roumanian Dances by Béla Bartók
Classical Symphony (First Movement) by Sergei Prokofiev
Dripsody by Hugh LeCaine
Carmina burana (Opening chorus) by Carl Orff
Bolero by Maurice Ravel
Short Ride in a Fast Machine by John Adams

Musical Elements:
aleatoric
atonality
expanded tonality
Expressionism
Impressionism
jazz influence
minimalism
modality
neo-Classicism
non-Western influences
pentatonic scale
polychords
polyrhythm
polytonality
post-Romanticism
serialism
technology
tone-row
whole-tone scale

Selection No. 1 ____________________ Composer ____________________

Musical features ____

____

____

____

Personal impressions ____

____

____

____

____

____

UNIT FIVE

Selection No. 2 ______________________ Composer ______________________

Musical features ______________________

____

____

____

Personal impressions ______________________

____

____

____

____

____

Selection No. 3 ______________________ Composer ______________________

Musical features ______________________

____

____

____

Personal impressions ______________________

____

____

____

____

____

Part Two: From your own repertoire, identify one work from the 20th century. Compile a list of the musical features that apply to your piece.

Title ______________________

Composer ______________________

Instrument ______________________

Musical features ______________________

____

____

____

UNIT FIVE

Debussy and Impressionism

The Life and Music of Claude Debussy (1862–1918)

Debussy is without a doubt the most influential French composer of the late-19th and early-20th centuries. His music reflects many features of late Romanticism, while also anticipating changes to come in the century ahead. As a young man, Debussy found inspiration in the luminous subtlety of the Impressionist painters, and in the sensuous, evocative works of the Symbolist poets. The Paris World Exposition of 1889 kindled his fascination with all things exotic. By assimilating all these influences, Debussy created a truly unique musical style.

Explain Debussy's connection to the following people, places, and events:

St.-Germaine-en-Laye ______________________________

Paris Conservatoire ______________________________

____

Prix de Rome ______________________________

____

Gabriel Fauré ______________________________

____

Erik Satie ______________________________

____

Richard Wagner ______________________________

____

Nadezhda von Meck ______________________________

____

Paris World Exposition, 1889 ______________________________

____

Maurice Maeterlinck ______________________________

____

La revue blanche ______________________________

____

Emma Bardac & Claude-Emma ("Chou Chou") ______________________

____

____

Maurice Ravel ______________________________________

____

Paris, 1918 ____

____

How did Debussy sign his manuscripts? ________________

Briefly explain the aesthetics of the Symbolist movement of the late-19th century and identify the main proponents of this style.

____

____

____

How did the artistic aims of these writers influence Debussy's compositional style?

____

____

WEB QUEST

View some Impressionist paintings on the internet. Using your search engine, type in key words like *Impressionism* and *Impressionist art*, or locate works by a specific artist, like Claude Monet. You can also find Impressionist artwork by visiting the official sites of museums like The Art Institute of Chicago, the Musée d'Orsay, and the Louvre.

For each of the following genres, list Debussy's contributions and innovations:

opera ____

other vocal works __________________________________

____

____

chamber music _____________________________________

____

____

ballet ______________________________

orchestral works ______________________________

____

____

piano music ______________________________

____

____

Required Listening: *Prélude à l'après-midi d'un faune*

Debussy conceived this work as an orchestral symphonic poem based on a beautiful poem by Mallarmé. Although it was written in 1894, *Prélude à l'après-midi d'un faune* exhibits musical characteristics that came to be identified with 20th-century style. In 1912, this work inspired Sergei Diaghilev, the famous artistic director and impresario, to create a new ballet. The daring new work was choreographed and danced by the legendary dancer, Vaslav Nijinsky.

Listen to a recording of *Prélude à l'après-midi d'un faune*. If possible, follow a score while you listen. Answer the following questions about the work, then complete the listening outline.

Translation of title ______________________________

Date of premiere ____________________ Genre ____________________

Form ____________________

What was the inspiration for this composition?

____

Briefly summarize the storyline of the poem.

____

____

____

____

There are some unique elements in this piece. Provide an explanation for each of the following:

antique cymbals ______________________________

____

glissando ____

____

faun ____

____

nymph ____

____

Debussy's scoring of this work marked a radical departure from conventional 19th-century practice. Use the chart below to indicate which instruments from each orchestral family he included in this work:

Strings	Woodwinds	Brass	Percussion
________	________	________	________
________	________		
________	________		
________	________		
________			

Describe the music for each section by commenting on the melody, harmony, rhythm, and use of instruments:

Section A

Ex. 5.1 Debussy, *Prélude à l'après-midi d'un faune,* opening theme.

Comments:

____

____

____

____

____

Section B

Ex. 5.2 Debussy, *Prélude à l'après-midi d'un faune,* Section B, new theme.

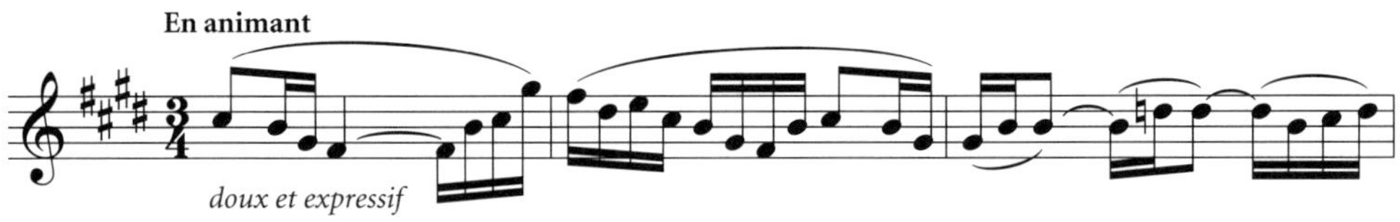

Ex. 5.3 Debussy, *Prélude à l'après-midi d'un faune,* Section B, contrasting theme.

Comments:

____

____

____

____

____

How does Section B contrast with Section A?

____

____

Section A^1 and Coda

Ex. 5.4 Debussy, *Prélude à l'après-midi d'un faune,* A^1 section, opening theme (modified).

Comments:

____

____

____

____

____

Using Ex. 5.1 and Ex. 5.4 as a reference, how has Section A been modified when it returns?

____

____

How did Debussy capture the dream-like atmosphere evoked in Mallarmé's poem?

___

Review the definition of Impressionism that you provided at the beginning of this unit. What parallels do you observe between the works of the Impressionist painters and the music of Debussy?

___

___

___

Recommended Listening for Debussy:
Préludes Book 1, no. 10, L 117 ("Sunken Cathedral")
Children's Corner Suite, L 113
Estampes
Beau soir
La mer, L 109

Debussy Works in *Celebration Series Perspectives®*:
The Little Shepherd (*Piano Repertoire 8*)
La fille aux cheveux de lin (*Piano Repertoire 9*)
Arabesque No. 1 (*Piano Repertoire 10*)
Study / Etude no. 12: *Etude No. 2* (*Piano Studies/Etudes 10*)

Stravinsky and His Ballets

The Life and Music of Igor Stravinsky (1882–1971)

When TIME magazine selected "people of the century" for its special Millennium 2000 issue, the classical musician chosen was Igor Stravinsky. His phenomenal career spanned the century and both revolutionized and defined stylistic trends. Stravinsky probably reached his widest audience as a result of his music being included in the Disney animated feature *Fantasia.*

Explain Stravinsky's connection to the following people, places, and events:

Oranienbaum ___

Feodor Stravinsky ___

___

Nikolai Rimsky-Korsakov ___

___

Sergei Diaghilev & Les Ballets Russes ___

___

___

Paris ______________________________

____

Pierre Monteux ______________________________

____

Switzerland ______________________________

____

Russian Revolution ______________________________

____

Jean Cocteau ______________________________

____

Pablo Picasso ______________________________

____

Harvard University ______________________________

____

Woody Herman ______________________________

____

Robert Craft ______________________________

____

California ______________________________

____

New York ______________________________

____

Island of San Michele, Venice ______________________________

Stravinsky's musical style encompasses a broad spectrum, from the post-Impressionism of his earliest works to the twelve-tone works of his later years. His career can be organized into four principal periods. Summarize the main stylistic currents that defined these four phases and name major compositions and genres for each.

The *Early Years (1882–1914)*

____

____

____

1. Title ________________ Genre ________________
2. Title ________________ Genre ________________

The *Transitional Years (1914–1920)*

____

____

____

1. Title ________________ Genre ________________
2. Title ________________ Genre ________________

The *Middle Years (1920–1954)*

____

____

____

1. Title ________________ Genre ________________
2. Title ________________ Genre ________________

The *Final Years (1954–1971)*

____

____

____

1. Title ________________ Genre ________________
2. Title ________________ Genre ________________

Building a Musical Vocabulary: *Stravinsky's Ballets*

Define the following terms:

ballet ____

____

____

choreographer ______

______

______

cadenza ______

______

______

"Petrushka chord" ______

______

______

primitivism ______

______

______

commedia dell'arte ______

______

______

Required Listening: Selections from *Petrushka* OR *The Rite of Spring*

Choose **EITHER** *Petrushka* **OR** *The Rite of Spring* and listen to a recording. If possible, follow a score while you listen, or watch a videotaped performance of the ballet. Answer the questions and complete the listening outline for the work you have chosen.

Petrushka

Petrushka was one in a long line of ground-breaking works created by Diaghilev and Les Ballets Russes. Audiences responded to the ballet's poignant story, vibrant color, and Russian folk elements.

When and where did this ballet premiere? year ______ city______

How were the individuals below connected to this work?

Sergei Diaghilev ______

______

Vaslav Nijinsky

Tamara Karsavina

Alexandre Benois

The Plot and Characters of *Petrushka*

Name the four principal characters in the story:

1. ____________ 3. ____________

2. ____________ 4. ____________

Summarize the action that takes place in each of the four scenes:

First Tableau Setting

Second Tableau Setting

Third Tableau Setting

Fourth Tableau Setting

UNIT FIVE

This ballet was innovative and highly original not only in terms of its music but also in its approach to choreography. Traditional 19th-century dance movements and gestures, as exhibited by the Ballerina, were juxtaposed with the interpretive leaping and flailing motions of Petrushka. Even though the Petrushka character originated in the comic tradition of the *commedia dell'arte*, in the end he lingers in our memory as a tragic and poignant figure.

First Tableau

For each of the three principal sections in this scene, refer to the Examples 5.5-5.11 as a guide, and summarize your observations about the music by answering the questions.

Section One: The Crowd Revels at the Shrovetide Fair

Tempo ____________________ Form ____________________

Ex. 5.5 Stravinsky, *Petrushka*/I, Section One: Crowd Scene.

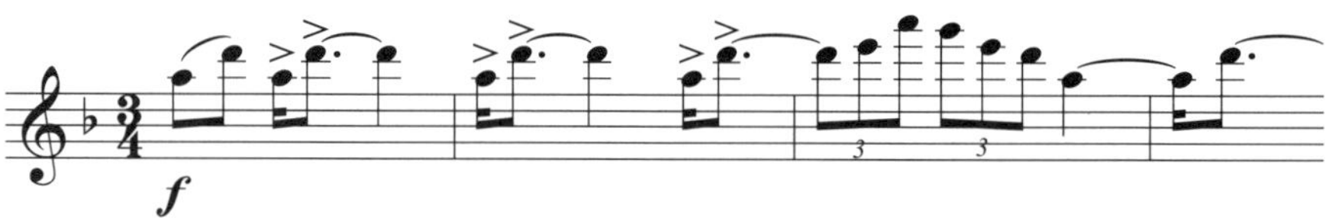

Ex. 5.6 Stravinsky, *Petrushka*/I, Section One: Song of the Volochebniki.

Ex. 5.7 Stravinsky, *Petrushka*/I, Section One: Hurdy-Gurdy Player.

Ex. 5.8 Stravinsky, *Petrushka*/I, Section One: Simple Dance Tune.

Describe the influence of folk music in Section One.

____

____

What scale type is employed in the Crowd Scene? ____________________

In what way was Stravinsky's approach to rhythm and meter innovative and daring for its time?

____

____

What harmonic devices does Stravinsky utilize in this section?

Comment on the colorful orchestration in this section.

What is a hurdy-gurdy and how is it evoked musically?

Section Two: The Arrival of the Showman

Tempo ____________________ Form ____________________

Ex. 5.9 Stravinsky, *Petrushka*/I, Section Two, The Showman's Cadenza.

By what means does the Showman bring the puppets to life?

How is an improvisatory character created in the cadenza?

How is the aura of mystery conveyed musically?

Section Three: The Puppets Come to Life

Tempo ______________________ Form ______________________

Ex. 5.10 Stravinsky, *Petrushka*/I, Section Three: Russian Dance.

Ex. 5.11 Stravinsky, *Petrushka*/I, Section Three: St. John's Eve Folksong.

What instrument (not usually included in the orchestra) is featured in this section?

____

Describe the texture and approach to harmony in this section.

____

____

____

How does the rhythm contribute to the animation of the characters?

____

____

____

The Rite of Spring

In the entire history of opening nights, the premiere of *The Rite of Spring* on May 29, 1913 at the *Théâtre des Champs Elysées* in Paris may very well be the most notorious. The unsuspecting audience was confronted by music and choreography that was stunning in its primal energy and raw physicality. Some were thrilled by this new and vital approach, while others felt threatened and insulted. Chaos and pandemonium erupted in the hall, and there were even a few physical confrontations.

What is the original French title of this work? ______________________

What connection did each of the following have to this work?

Sergei Diaghilev ______________________________

____

Nicolas Roerich ______________________________

____

Vaslav Nijinsky ______________________________

____

Les Ballets Russes ______________________________

____

Pierre Monteux ______________________________

____

The Plot and Characters of *The Rite of Spring*

This ballet is divided into two main parts. The descriptions below are drawn from a letter by Roerich to Diaghilev before the first performance:

Part One — The Adoration of the Earth

"My intention is that the first set should transport us to the foot of a sacred hill, in a lush plain, where Slavonic tribes are gathered together to celebrate the spring rites. In this scene there is an old witch, who predicts the future, a marriage by capture, round dances. The wise elder is brought from the village to imprint his sacred kiss on the new-flowering earth. During this rite the crowd is seized with a mystic terror…"

Part Two — The Sacrifice

"Young virgins dance in circles on the sacred hill amid enchanted rocks; then they choose the victim they intend to honor. In a moment she will dance her last dance before the ancients clad in bearskins to show that the bear was man's ancestor. Then the greybeards dedicate the victim to the God Yarilo."

Part Two (Selections)

Dance of the Chosen One (Naming and Honoring of the Chosen One)

Tempo ______________________________

Approach to meter ____

Ex. 5.12 Stravinsky, *Rite of Spring,* Part Two: Dance of the Chosen One.

The striking primitivism that characterizes this ballet is achieved in this section through various musical means. Prominent features in this section include:

- an expanded percussion section
- special effects by other instruments
- pounding accents
- extreme contrasts in dynamics and articulation.

The terms listed below are found in Stravinsky's original score. What do they ask the performers to do?

pizz. ____

arco ____

secco ____

gliss. ____

flatterz. ____

pavillons en l'air ____________________________________

Complete the statements below by circling the letter next to the correct answer:

The opening gesture consists of:
a) *glissandi* played by woodwind instruments in high registers
b) lyrical melody in the strings
c) oboe solo

The rhythmic structure includes:
a) free, unmeasured rhythm
b) lilting waltz rhythm
c) shifting meters and accents

The harmonic language is best characterized as:
a) boldly dissonant
b) purely diatonic
c) lush and romantic

The composer breaks with tradition by using the string section:
a) in a brittle, percussive manner
b) in broad sweeping lines
c) in symmetrical dance rhythms

The approach to dynamics is:
a) restrained and cautious
b) extreme in its contrasts
c) predictable and uniform

The character of this section can be described as:
a) calm and serene
b) turbulent and virile
c) playful and coy

Evocation of the Ancestors

Ex. 5.13 Stravinsky, *The Rite of Spring,* Part Two: Evocation of the Ancestors.

How does the opening of this section create contrast with the preceding section?

What is the predominant musical texture here?

a) monophonic
b) polyphonic
c) homophonic/chordal

Bassoons and contra-bassoons provide a brief descending flourish that serves as a bridge to the next section, marked *Lento* in the score.

Ritual Action of the Ancestors

Ex. 5.14 Stravinsky, *The Rite of Spring,* Part Two: Ritual Action of the Ancestors.

Complete the following statements about The Ritual Action of the Ancestors by circling the letter next to the correct answer:

Against a constant quarter note pulsation, a melodic dialogue occurs between:

a) French horn and trombone
b) flute and clarinet
c) English horn and flute

The principal theme in Ex. 5.14 is introduced by:

a) trombones and bass trombones
b) violins and violas
c) flutes and clarinets

Accompanying "swirling" figures occur in:

a) horns
b) violins
c) flutes

Toward the end of the movement, percussion instruments become more prominent in the orchestration. Describe their participation.

Sacrificial Dance of the Chosen One
In this final scene—the culmination of the ballet—the music and choreography reach their frenzied climax. This is the only section in the entire ballet that features a solo dancer, the young woman who is to be sacrificed to ensure the fertility of the earth. Through the dense orchestral writing, the relentless rhythmic pounding, unprecedented use of changing meter, and dissonant harmonic language, a powerful scene of pagan ritual is fully realized.

To complete your study of *The Rite of Spring*, listen to *Sacrificial Dance of the Chosen One*. Write your reactions below.

How is primitivism realized in this ballet?

In what way was Stravinsky's approach to rhythm and meter innovative and daring for its time?

Throughout the ages, literature, visual arts, and music have often elicited controversy, as was the case with *The Rite of Spring*. Think of one recent example from your own experience where an artistic work has stimulated strong reaction and opinions. Describe the work, the controversy surrounding it, and your own viewpoint.

Recommended Listening for Stravinsky:

The Firebird
L'Histoire du Soldat
Symphony of Psalms
Ebony Concerto
The Owl and the Pussycat

Leonard Bernstein and *West Side Story*

The Life and Music of Leonard Bernstein (1918–1990)

Leonard Bernstein displayed a versatility and personal magnetism that made him a larger-than-life figure in American music circles. In his career, he pursued many avenues as a conductor, pianist, recording artist, composer, and educator. *West Side Story* has become an American classic. Its songs and dances are symbols of the American social and cultural mosaic.

Explain Bernstein's connections to the following:

Lawrence, Massachusetts __________

New England Conservatory __________

Harvard University __________

Walter Piston and Edward Burlingame Hill __________

Curtis Institute __________

Serge Koussevitsky __________

Tanglewood Festival __________

New York Philharmonic __________

Jerome Robbins __________

Felicia Montealegre __________

Vienna Philharmonic __________

Young People's Concerts __________

Identify the genre of each of the following important works by Bernstein:

Candide __________

UNIT FIVE

The Age of Anxiety ____________________

Kaddish ____________________

Fancy Free ____________________

A Quiet Place ____________________

On the Waterfront ____________________

Building a Musical Vocabulary: *The American Musical*

Explain the following terms:

operetta ____________________

vaudeville ____________________

Broadway musical ____________________

Off-Broadway ____________________

jazz ____________________

lyricist ____________________

verse-chorus ____________________

ostinato ____

____

hemiola ____

____

____

mambo ____

____

cha-cha ____

____

brass "shakes" ____

____

Name two famous American composer/lyricist teams who collaborated successfully to produce Broadway musicals, and name two of their works:

1. ____________________ & ____________________

Titles ____________________ ____________________

2. ____________________ & ____________________

Titles ____________________ ____________________

Name one contemporary Broadway composer who also writes all of his own lyrics, and name two of his works:

1. ____________________ 2. ____________________

The Plot and Characters of *West Side Story*

West Side Story is a brilliant adaptation of Shakespeare's famous tragedy, *Romeo and Juliet*. The longstanding feud between the two Renaissance Italian families in Shakespeare's play is transformed into tensions between two rival gangs on the Upper West Side of New York City in the 1950s.

When did *West Side Story* premiere on Broadway? ____________________

UNIT FIVE

What contribution did each of these individuals make to the creation of this work?

Leonard Bernstein ______________________________

Arthur Laurents ______________________________

Stephen Sondheim ______________________________

Jerome Robbins ______________________________

Harold Prince ______________________________

WEB QUEST

Are you familiar with Shakespeare's *Romeo and Juliet*? Use the internet to learn more about this famous play. You can find plot summaries, descriptions of characters, thematic discussions, and much more. In your search engine, try combining *Romeo and Juliet* with *West Side Story* to find comparisons between the two works.

Provide a brief summary of the original *Romeo and Juliet* plot.

____

____

____

____

____

____

____

Listed below are the principal characters in *West Side Story* and *Romeo and Juliet*. Wherever possible, equate the character in the musical with his/her counterpart in Shakespeare's original tragedy:

***West Side Story* Characters:**

The Jets (= ______________)

Riff (= ______________)

Tony (= ______________)

The Sharks (= ______________)

Bernardo (= ______________)

Chino (= ______________)

Maria (= ______________)

Anita (= ______________)

Additional Characters:

Doc (= ____________________)

Officer Krupke (= ____________________)

***Romeo and Juliet* Characters:**

The Montagues	The Capulets	Additional Characters
Romeo	Juliet	Prince Escalus
Mercutio	Tybalt	Friar Laurence
	Nurse	Paris

Can you find any other parallels? ____

____

How do the fates of the two heroines (Maria and Juliet) differ? ____________________

____

Summarize the action that unfolds in the two acts of *West Side Story:*

Act One Setting (opening scene) ______________________________________

____

____

____

____

____

____

____

____

Act Two Setting (opening scene) ______________________________________

____

____

____

____

____

____

____

____

Required Listening: Selections from *West Side Story*

Listen to a recording of *West Side Story,* or watch the 1961 Oscar-winning movie starring Natalie Wood. If possible, follow a score while you listen. Choose **TWO** musical numbers from the list below, and complete a musical description of each.

Tonight Ensemble
Maria
Dance at the Gym
I Feel Pretty
America

Selection No. 1

Title ______________________________

Character(s) singing ______________________________

Setting ______________________________

What sentiments are being expressed?

____

____

____

____

melody ______________________________

____

____

harmony ______________________________

____

____

texture ______________________________

____

rhythm/meter ______________________________

____

____

use of instruments ______________________________

____

____

special features (exotic elements, recurring motives, etc.)

Selection No. 2

Title

Character(s) singing

Setting

What sentiments are being expressed?

melody

harmony

texture

rhythm/meter

use of instruments

UNIT FIVE

special features (exotic elements, recurring motives, etc.)

Now that you have learned about opera (*Carmen, Madama Butterfly*) and the American musical (*West Side Story*), what similarities and differences do you observe between the two genres?

Similarities

Differences

Recommended Listening for Bernstein:
Overture and "Glitter and be Gay" to *Candide*
Anniversaries for Piano
Symphony No. 3, "Kaddish"
On the Waterfront

Bernstein Works in *Celebration Series Perspectives®*:
For Susanna Kyle (*Piano Repertoire 6*)

Alexina Louie and the Canadian Contemporary Music Scene

The Life and Music of Alexina Louie (1949–)

Alexina Louie has garnered an international reputation with her kaleidoscopic music. Her compositional style encompasses both traditional and innovative contemporary features, and fuses European and Asian influences. Louie's works reflect a growing interest in pan-ethnic music, a trend represented by composers Tan Dun, Toru Takemitsu, and Christos Hatzis.

WEB QUEST

Use the internet to learn more about Alexina Louie and her music. Try searching using her name, as well as the Canadian Music Centre, *Thunder Dragon,* and *Music for Piano.* To learn more about musical activities and trends in Canada, visit the official website of the Canadian Broadcasting Corporation (CBC) or simply search on *Canadian music.*

Explain Louie's connections to the following:

Vancouver ______________________

The Royal Conservatory of Music ______________________

University of British Columbia ______________________

University of California at San Diego ______________________

Pauline Oliveros ______________________

Alex Pauk ______________________

Esprit Orchestra ______________________

Vancouver World Exposition, 1986 ______________________

Glenn Gould ______________________

Juno Award ______________________

SOCAN Award ______________________

University of Calgary ______________________

Jules Leger Prize ______________________

David Henry Hwang ______________________

Name two compositions by Alexina Louie in each of the following areas:

keyboard	____________	____________
chamber works	____________	____________
orchestra	____________	____________
film scores	____________	____________
vocal	____________	____________
electronic	____________	____________

UNIT FIVE

Identify the following Canadian performers and ensembles, and name one composition by Louie that each premiered:

	Instrument	Composition Title
Joseph Macerollo	____________	____________
Robert Aitken	____________	____________
Jon Kimura Parker	____________	____________
Angela Hewitt	____________	____________
Orford String Quartet	____________	____________
Beverley Johnston	____________	____________
Erica Goodman	____________	____________

Throughout her career, Louie has received many commissions from leading orchestras. Identify one composition premiered by each of the following orchestras:

	Conductor	Composition Title
Vancouver Symphony Orchestra	____________	____________
Toronto Symphony Orchestra	____________	____________
Manitoba Chamber Orchestra	____________	____________
Ensemble SMCQ	____________	____________
Esprit Orchestra	____________	____________

UNIT FIVE

Required Listening: "Distant Memories" from *Music for Piano* OR "Thunder Dragon" from *Music for Heaven and Earth*

"Distant Memories" from *Music for Piano*

"Distant Memories" is the third of four pieces in the collection *Music for Piano*. This work was commissioned by the Alliance for Canadian New Music Projects in 1982. You may enjoy listening to all four of these short pieces before completing the listening outline for "Distant Memories." The titles are as follows:

The Enchanted Bells
Changes
Distant Memories
Once upon a time

Listen to a recording of "Distant Memories." Follow a score while you listen. (This piece is in the *Celebration Series©, The Piano Odyssey©, Piano Repertoire 9.*)

The following terms are used in "Distant Memories." Provide a definition for each:

senza misura ______________________________

quasi berceuse ______________________________

perdendosi ______________________________

The organization of this work can be loosely regarded as a ternary form. The *senza misura* measures at the beginning and the end serve to frame the metered middle section.

A	m. 1	*senza misura*
B	mm. 2-35	*quasi berceuse–più mosso–a tempo*
A^1	mm. 36-end	*senza misura*

Section A

How does the composer suggest in the score an improvisatory style for this opening passage? Does the performance you listened to have this quality?

What unusual notation does Louie use to indicate *accelerandi*? Draw an example below:

The composer guides the performer's interpretation by indicating the appropriate duration in seconds at the end of each system.

In light of the title, what memories or images are conjured for you by this opening section?

Section B

Outline how Louie achieves contrast in this section by describing her treatment of the following elements:

rhythm ______________________________

UNIT FIVE

texture ____

____

____

tempo ____

____

____

harmony ____

____

____

Describe the change that occurs at m. 10.

____

____

____

How do these musical changes evoke a different character and atmosphere? What memories do you think the composer is depicting here?

____

____

____

Compared to many piano works of this era, "Distant Memories" encompasses a relatively narrow keyboard range. Examine the score to find the lowest and highest notes.

Highest note ____________________ Lowest note ____________________

What musical and technical challenges does this piece present to the pianist?

____

____

____

"Thunder Dragon" from *Music for Heaven and Earth*

This colorful orchestral work represents a popular trend from the final decades of the 20th century: a synthesis of Western classical and Eastern traditional elements. Alexina Louie draws from her Chinese heritage and the influence of 20th-century composers such as Olivier Messiaen, Igor Stravinsky, Béla Bartók, and John Adams.

What is the date of this composition? ____________________

In the preface to the score of *Music for Heaven and Earth*, Louie described the work as follows:

> "Because *Music for Heaven and Earth* is to be taken on the Toronto Symphony Pacific Rim tour a few days after its premiere in Toronto, the work offered me a unique opportunity to reach out to a large part of the world in a very direct and immediate way. It also offered me the opportunity to continue to explore the elements of my musical language (an integration of oriental musical concepts and Western art music) in a large orchestral context. Echoes of Gagaku music (Imperial court music of Japan) are heard in Procession of Celestial Deities and elements of Peking opera summon the Thunder Dragon."

The one-movement *Music for Heaven and Earth* (for large orchestra) is in five continuous sections. You may enjoy listening to the complete work. The sections are as follows:

1. Procession of Celestial Deities
2. Thunder Dragon
3. The Void
4. Earthrise
5. River of Stars

The large orchestra specified in the title requires four percussionists to use a myriad of eastern and western instruments. Among them are:

Western: glockenspiel, vibraphone, piano, timpani
Eastern: kabuki blocks, lion's roar, Japanese temple bowls

Listen to a recording of "Thunder Dragon." If possible, follow a score while you listen. Answer the questions below:

By what musical means does Louie establish an atmosphere of ceremony

and ritual? ____________________

____

Comment on the effect of the following:

fortissimo opening chord ____________________

brass fanfare figures ____________________

____

____

____

UNIT FIVE

Throughout the opening section, the meter is constantly shifting ($\frac{4}{4}$, $\frac{5}{4}$, $\frac{4}{4}$, $\frac{2}{4}$, etc.). What other work have you studied that features changing meters?

Describe the use of percussion instruments. List specific instruments you can discern or recognize, and comment on the effects they create.

Even non-percussion instruments can be used percussively. How is this approach explored in "Thunder Dragon"?

Throughout the work, do you perceive the instruments individually, or are they treated as families or sections? Comment specifically on Louie's treatment of the following:

strings

woodwinds

brass

UNIT FIVE

Finally, consider the following quote from Ms. Louie:

> "For a number of years now my music has been influenced by the great power and the beauty of nature and man's responsibility to preserve and cherish it. *Music for Heaven and Earth* is the embodiment of my feelings of wonder, fear, and awe of the vast, mysterious, black void of outer space, love and tenderness at the sight of our rising, beautiful, fragile earth from the desolate surface of the moon, and finally, a celebration of our unique place in the starry heavens."

Do you think she has achieved her objectives? Why or why not?

Recommended Listening for Alexina Louie:
Music for a Small Planet
Music from Night's Edge
Scenes from a Jade Terrace
O Magnum Mysterium

Louie Works in *Celebration Series Perspectives®*:
O Moon (*Piano Repertoire 8*)
Distant Memories (*Piano Repertoire 9*)

Now that you have sampled several compositions from the 20th century, comment on the following features of 20th-century style as they relate to specific composers and works:

new approaches to rhythm ______________________________

____

harmonic language ______________________________

____

influence of non-Western music ______________________________

____

technological innovations ______________________________

____

innovative orchestration ______________________________

____

Review and Reflection

What do *you* like best about 20th-century music? Do you have a favorite composer or piece from this era? Of the works you studied in this unit, which did you enjoy the most, and why?

____

____

____

____

UNIT FIVE

Quiz

1. Name one 20th-century composer associated with each of the following:

   St. Petersburg ______________________________

   Prix de Rome ______________________________

   Vancouver ______________________________

   Les Ballets Russes ______________________________

   St. Germain-en-Laye ______________________________

   Juno Award ______________________________

   Paris World Exposition ______________________________

   Claude-Emma (Chou-Chou) ______________________________

   California ______________________________

   Robert Craft ______________________________

2. Choose the answer that best completes each of the following statements:

   Stephane Mallarmé was a celebrated:
   a) Impressionist painter
   b) Symbolist poet
   c) choreographer

   The "Petrushka chord" combines:
   a) C major and F sharp major triads
   b) C major and C minor triads
   c) dominant and diminished seventh chords

   West Side Story was inspired by:
   a) *Romeo and Juliet*
   b) *A Midsummer Night's Dream*
   c) *Much Ado About Nothing*

   Folk melodies are quoted in:
   a) *West Side Story*
   b) *Petrushka*
   c) *Prélude à l'après-midi d'un faune*

   Dances in *West Side Story* include:
   a) *habañera* and samba
   b) mambo and cha-cha
   c) meringue and salsa

   "Thunder Dragon" by Alexina Louie makes use of:
   a) fanfare figures
   b) expanded percussion section
   c) horn glissandi
   d) all of the above

UNIT FIVE

The opening theme of *Prélude à l'après-midi d'un faune* is played by:	a) English horn b) clarinet c) flute
The instrumentation of *Petrushka* includes:	a) piano b) organ c) harpsichord
The closing scene in *The Rite of Spring* is called:	a) Adoration of the Earth b) Song of the Volochebniki c) Sacrificial Dance
In the *Prélude à l'après-midi d'un faune,* the percussion section is:	a) expanded b) reduced c) eliminated
The structural design of *Prélude à l'après-midi d'un faune* is:	a) sonata-allegro form b) modified ternary c) rondo
The lyricist for *West Side Story* was:	a) Jerome Robbins b) Stephen Sondheim c) William Shakespeare

Appendices

APPENDIX A – RECOMMENDED RESOURCES

Dictionaries and Encyclopedias

Chwialkowski, Jerzy. *The Da Capo Catalogue of Classical Music Compositions.* New York: Da Capo Press, 1996.

Kallman, Helmut, Gilles Potvin, and Kenneth Winters, eds. *Encyclopedia of Music in Canada.* 2nd ed. Toronto: University of Toronto Press, 1992.

Kennedy, Michael, ed. *The Concise Oxford Dictionary of Music.* 4th ed. London: Oxford University Press, 1996.

Kennedy, Michael, ed. *The Oxford Dictionary of Music.* 2nd ed. London: Oxford University Press, 1995.

Randel, Don Michael, ed. *The Harvard Concise Dictionary of Music and Musicians.* Cambridge, Massachusetts: Belknap Press of Harvard University Press, 1999.

Randel, Don Michael, ed. *The New Harvard Dictionary of Music.* Cambridge, Massachusetts: Harvard University Press, 1986.

Sadie, Stanley, ed. *The New Grove Dictionary of Music and Musicians.* 2nd ed. 29 vols. London: Macmillan, 2001.

Sadie, Stanley, ed. *The New Grove Dictionary of Opera.* 4 vols. London: Macmillan, 1992.

Sadie, Stanley, ed. *The Norton/Grove Concise Encyclopedia of Music.* New York: W.W. Norton, 1988.

Slonimsky, Nicholas. *Baker's Biographical Dictionary of Musicians.* 8th ed. New York: Schirmer, 1984.

Slonimsky, Nicholas, and Laura Diane Kuhn. *Baker's Biographical Dictionary of Musicians.* 6 vols. Centennial ed. New York: Schirmer, 2001.

Westrup, Jack Allan et al. *The New College Encyclopedia of Music.* New York: W.W. Norton, 1981.

General Texts

Abraham, Gerald, ed. *The Concise Oxford History of Music.* London: Oxford University Press, 1985.

Grout, Donald Jay, and Claude V. Palisca. *A History of Western Music.* 6th ed. New York: W.W. Norton, 2001.

Hanning, Barbara Russanno. *A Concise History of Western Music.* 2nd ed. New York: W.W. Norton, 2002.

Holoman, D. Kern. *Masterworks: A Musical Discovery.* 2nd ed. Upper Saddle River, New Jersey: Prentice Hall, 2001.

Machlis, Joseph, and Kristine Forney. *The Enjoyment of Music.* 9th ed. New York: W.W. Norton, 2002.

Schonberg, Harold C. *Lives of the Great Composers.* 3rd ed. New York: W.W. Norton, 1997.

Stolba, K. Marie. *The Development of Western Music: A History.* 3rd ed. Boston: McGraw-Hill, 1998.

Yudkin, Jeremy. *Understanding Music.* Upper Saddle River, New Jersey: Prentice Hall, 1999.

Baroque Period Texts

Boyd, Malcolm. *J.S. Bach.* London: Oxford University Press, 1999.

Bukofzer, Manfred. *Music in the Baroque Era: From Monteverdi to Bach.* New York: W.W. Norton, 1947.

David, Hans T., and Arthur Mendel, eds. *The New Bach Reader.* Revised and enlarged by Christoph Wolff. New York: W.W. Norton, 1999.

Hogwood, Christopher. *Handel.* New York: W.W. Norton, 1996.

Landon, H.C. Robbins. *Handel and His World.* Boston: Little, Brown, 1984.

Palisca, Claude V. *Baroque Music.* 3rd ed. Englewood Cliffs, New Jersey: Prentice Hall, 1991.

Talbot, Michael. *Vivaldi.* London: J.M. Dent and Sons, 1978.

Wolff, Christoph. *Johann Sebastian Bach: The Learned Musician.* New York: W.W. Norton, 2000.

Wolff, Christoph. *The World of the Bach Cantatas.* New York: W.W. Norton, 1997.

Classical Period Texts

Cooper, Barry. *The Beethoven Compendium: A Guide to Beethoven's Life and Music.* New York: W.W. Norton, 1996.

Deutsch, Otto Erich. *Mozart: A Documentary Biography.* Stanford: Stanford University Press, 1991.

Downs, Philip G. *Classical Music: The Era of Haydn, Mozart and Beethoven.* New York: W.W. Norton, 1992.

Geiringer, Karl. *Haydn: A Creative Life in Music.* 3rd ed., revised and expanded. Berkeley: University of California Press, 1983.

Hamburger, Michael, ed. *Beethoven's Letters, Journals, and Conversations.* New York: W.W. Norton, 1992.

Kerman, Joseph, Alan Tyson, et al. *The New Grove Beethoven.* New York: W.W. Norton, 1997.

Landon, H.C. Robbins. *Haydn: The Early Years, 1732-1765.* New York: W.W. Norton, 1995.

Landon, H.C. Robbins. *Haydn: At Esterházy, 1766-1790.* New York: W.W. Norton, 1995.

Landon, H.C. Robbins. *Haydn in England, 1791-1795.* New York: W.W. Norton, 1995.

Landon, H.C. Robbins. *Haydn: The Years of "The Creation."* New York: W.W. Norton, 1995.

Landon, H.C. Robbins. *Haydn: The Late Years, 1801-1809.* New York: W.W. Norton, 1995.

Pauly, Reinhard G. *Music in the Classic Period.* 4th ed. Upper Saddle River, New Jersey: Prentice Hall, 2000.

Ratner, Leonard G. *Classic Music: Expression, Form and Style.* New York: Schirmer, 1980.

Rosen, Charles. *The Classical Style: Haydn, Mozart and Beethoven.* Expanded edition. New York: W.W. Norton, 1998.

Solomon, Maynard. *Mozart: A Life.* New York: Harper Collins Publishers, 1995.

Solomon, Maynard. *Beethoven.* New York: Schirmer Books, 1977.

Spaethling, Robert, ed. *Mozart's Letters, Mozart's Life: Selected Letters.* New York: W.W. Norton, 2000.

Zaslaw, Neal, and William Cowdery, eds. *The Complete Mozart: A Guide to the Musical Works of Wolfgang Amadeus Mozart.* New York: W.W. Norton, 1990.

Romantic Period Texts

Atwood, William G. *Fryderyk Chopin: Pianist from Warsaw.* New York: Columbia University Press, 1987.

Barzun, Jacques. *Berlioz and His Century: An Introduction to the Age of Romanticism.* Chicago: University of Chicago Press, 1982.

Brown, Maurice J.E., and Eric Sams. *The New Grove Schubert.* New York: W.W. Norton, 1997.

Dean, Winton. *Georges Bizet: His Life and His Work.* London: J.M. Dent and Sons, 1948; 3rd ed., 1975.

Deutsch, Otto Erich. *The Schubert Reader: A Life of Franz Schubert in Letters and Documents.* New York: W.W. Norton, 1977.

Einstein, Alfred. *Music in the Romantic Era.* New York: W.W. Norton, 1947.

Holoman, D. Kern. *Berlioz: A Musical Biography of the Creative Genius of the Romantic Era.* Cambridge, Massachusetts: Harvard University Press, 1989.

Longyear, Rey M. *Nineteenth-Century Romanticism in Music.* Englewood Cliffs, New Jersey: Prentice Hall, 3rd ed., 1988.

Macdonald, Hugh, ed. *Selected Letters of Berlioz.* New York: W.W. Norton, 1997.

Rosen, Charles. *The Romantic Generation.* (with CD) Cambridge, Massachusetts: Harvard University Press, 1995.

Samson, Jim. *The Music of Chopin.* Oxford: Oxford University Press, 1994.

Walker, Alan, ed. *The Chopin Companion.* New York: W.W. Norton, 1973.

Zamoyski, Adam. *Chopin: A New Biography.* Garden City, New York: Doubleday, 1980.

20th-century Texts

Burton, Humphrey. *Leonard Bernstein.* New York: Anchor Books, 1995.

Craft, Robert. *Stravinsky: Glimpses of a Life.* New York: St. Martin's Press, 1992.

Kostka, Stefan. *Materials and Techniques of Twentieth-Century Music.* 2nd ed. Englewood Cliffs, New Jersey: Prentice Hall, 1999.

Lockspeiser, Edward. *Debussy.* London: J.M. Dent and Sons, 1936; rev. ed., 1963.

Machlis, Joseph. *An Introduction to Contemporary Music.* 2nd ed. New York: W.W. Norton, 1979.

Myers, Paul. *Leonard Bernstein.* New York: Phaidon Press, 1998.

Proctor, George A. *Canadian Music of the Twentieth Century.* Toronto: University of Toronto Press, 1980.

Salzman, Eric. *Twentieth Century Music: An Introduction.* 4th ed. Englewood Cliffs, New Jersey: Prentice Hall, 2002.

Stravinsky, Igor. *An Autobiography.* New York: W.W. Norton, 1998.

Stravinsky, Vera, and Robert Craft. *Stravinsky in Pictures and Documents.* New York: Simon and Schuster, 1978.

Watkins, Glenn. *Soundings: Music in the Twentieth Century.* New York: Schirmer, 1988.

Internet Resources (General Sites)

Worldwide Internet Music Resources: www.music.indiana.edu/music_resources

Sibelius Academy Music Resources: www.siba.fi/Kulttuuripalvelut/music.html

The Classical Music Pages: www.rz-berlin.mpg.de/cmp/classmus.html

Classical Net: www.classical.net

Listen (Kerman/Tomlinson): www.bedfordstmartins.com/listen

VHS Video Resources

The Famous Composers Series. (Distributed by KULTUR) Written, produced, and directed by Malcolm Hossick. Titles include: *Johann Sebastian Bach, Ludwig van Beethoven, Joseph Haydn, Wolfgang Amadeus Mozart, Giacomo Puccini, Franz Schubert, Igor Stravinsky.*

A & E "Biography" Series. (Distributed by New Video) Titles include: *Mozart and Beethoven: The Sound and The Fury, The Story of the Symphony.* With André Previn and The Royal Philharmonic. Six-part Series. Vol. 1: Haydn and Mozart, Vol. 2: Beethoven, Vol. 3: Berlioz. (Distributed by Kultur)

HANDEL: *Messiah*
Neville Marriner, Academy and Chorus of St. Martin-in-the-Fields, McNair, Otter, Chance, Hadley; Philips 440 070 5323.

BEETHOVEN: *Symphony No. 5*
Leonard Bernstein, Vienna Philharmonic; DG 44007 32043.

SCHUBERT: *Lieder*
Dietrich Fischer-Dieskau; Warner 6 3984 23031 3 2.

CHOPIN: *Selections*
Lazar Berman; Kultur 1 56127 428 1.

BERLIOZ: *Symphonie fantastique*
John Eliot Gardiner, Orchestre Revolutionaire et Romantique Philips 440 070 254 3.

BIZET: *Carmen*
Film version, directed by P. Rosi; Lorin Maazel, Orchestre National de France, with Migenes, Domingo, Esham, Raimondi, Columbia 60487.

BERNSTEIN: *West Side Story*
Bernstein conducts, with Te Kanawa, Troyanos, Carreras; DG 072 206 B GVG.

Film Version, directed by Robert Wise and Jerome Robbins, starring Natalie Wood. MGM Musicals 0 7928 65295 3.

DVD Video Resources

VIVALDI: *The Four Seasons*
Nigel Kennedy; EMI 7243 4 92499 9 8.

Anne-Sophie Mutter, solo violin, Herbert von Karajan, Berlin Philharmonic, Sony Classical 1 57330 135 3.

HANDEL: *Messiah*
King's College Choir, Stephane Cleoburg, Brandenburg Consort. RM 14381 5815 2.

J.S. BACH: *The Well-Tempered Clavier, 48 Preludes and Fugues*
Hewitt, MacGregor, Demidenko, Gavrilov [each plays 12]. Studio Image Entertainment.

BEETHOVEN: *Symphony No. 5*
Karajan, Berlin Philharmonic; Sony Classical 1 57330 135 3.

The Story of the Symphony; narrated and conducted by André Previn, with the Royal Philharmonia Orchestra; RM Arts/Image Entertainment.

BERLIOZ: *Symphonie fantastique*
The Story of the Symphony; Previn, Royal Philharmonia Orchestra. RM Arts/Image Entertainment ID 5818RADVD.

John Eliot Gardiner, Orchestre Revolutionaire et Romantique; Philips.

BIZET: *Carmen*
James Levine, Metropolitan Opera, Baltsa, Carreras, Mitchell, Ramey; DG 0730009.

Zubin Mehta, Covent Garden, Ewing, Lima, Vadura, Quilico RM 14381 5782 2.

Cast of the Rosi film version: Lorin Maazel, Orchestre National de France, Migenes, Domingo. Esham, Raimondi; Columbia.

PUCCINI: *Madama Butterfly*
Cast of the Mitterand film version: James Conlon, conductor, with Ying Huang, Troxell; Columbia.

Maazel, Teatro Alla Scala, Hayashi, Kim, Dvorsky; Studio Image Entertainment.

Karajan, Freni, Domingo, Ludwig; directed by Ponelle; Decca.

DEBUSSY: *Prélude à l'aprés-midi d'un faune*
Karajan, Berlin Philharmonic, Sony Classical 0 7389 1923.

APPENDIX B – RECOMMENDED LISTENING MATERIALS

The following is a list of suggested recordings for each of the required pieces discussed in this volume:

Britten, Benjamin. *The Young Person's Guide to the Orchestra*
- Minnesota Orchestra, conducted by Neville Marriner, EMI CDC 7 49300-2
- New York Philharmonic Orchestra, conducted by Leonard Bernstein, Sony 7464 46712-2
- London Symphony Orchestra, conducted by Benjamin Britten, London 417 509-2

Vivaldi, Antonio. *The Four Seasons*, op. 8
- Il Giardino Armonico, conducted by Giovanni Antonini, Teldec 4509 97971-2
- English Concert, conducted by Trevor Pinnock, CRD 3325
- Tafelmusik, conducted by Jeanne Lamon, Sony SK 48251
- Drottningholm Baroque Ensemble, BIS CD 275
- I Solisti Veneti, conducted by Claudio Scimone, Erato 4509 99666
- English Chamber Orchestra, soloist, Kennedy, EMI CDC 56253
- Raglan Baroque Players, conducted by Nicholas Kraemer, Virgin CDVB 61668

Handel, George Frideric. *Messiah*
- Les Arts Florissants, conducted by William Christie, HMX 2901498.99
- Monteverdi Choir, English Baroque Soloists, conducted by John Eliot Gardiner, Philips 434 297-2
- Toronto Mendelssohn Choir, Toronto Symphony, conducted by Andrew Davis, EMI CDC-7 49027 2
- Taverner Choir and Players, conducted by Andrew Parrott, Virgin Veritas 5620042
- The English Concert and Choir, conducted by Trevor Pinnock, DG Archiv 423 630

Bach, Johann Sebastian. *The Well-Tempered Clavier*
- Glenn Gould, Sony SM2K 52600, SM2K 52603
- Angela Hewitt, Hyperion CDA 67301/2, CDA 67303/4
- Rosalyn Tureck, DG 463 305
- Ralph Kirkpatrick, DG Archiv 463 601 2
- Kenneth Gilbert, DG Archiv 413 439
- Andras Schiff, Decca 414 388
- Keith Jarrett, ECM 835246

Haydn, Franz Joseph. *String Quartets*, op. 76, "Erdödy"
- Tokyo String Quartet, Sony SB2K 53522
- Amadeus Quartet, DG 415 867-2
- Alban Berg Quartet, EMI CDC5 56166 2
- Kodaly Quartet, Naxos 8 550314, 8 550315
- Lindsay Quartet, ASV CD DCA 1076, 1077

Mozart, Wolfgang Amadeus. *Eine kleine Nachtmusik*, K 525
- Wiener Mozart Ensemble 4, Willi Boskovsky, Decca 443 458 2
- I Musici de Montréal, conducted by Yuli Turovsky, Chandos CHAN 9045
- Academy of St. Martin-In-the-Fields, conducted by Neville Marriner, Decca 433634

Beethoven, Ludwig van. *Symphony No. 5*
- Berlin Philharmonic Orchestra, conducted by Herbert von Karajan, DG 419 051-2, DG 439 004-2
- Concertgebouw, conducted by Wolfgang Sawallisch, EMI 73326-2
- Leipzig Gewandhaus Orchestra, conducted by Kurt Masur, Philips 434 156 2
- Chicago Symphony Orchestra, conducted by Sir George Solti, Decca 443 756-2
- Cleveland Orchestra, conducted by George Szell, Sony Ess. SBK 47651
- Cleveland Orchestra, conducted by Christoph Von Dohnanyi, Telarc 80163
- Philadelphia Orchestra, conducted by Eugene Ormandy, Sony 63266
- Wiener Philharmoniker, conducted by Carlos Kleiber, DG 415 861-2GH
- Münchner Philharmoniker, conducted by Sergiu Celibidache, EMI 7243 5 56837 2
- Orchestre Revolutionnaire et Romantique, conducted by John Eliot Gardiner, DG Archiv 439 900

Schubert, Franz. (Lieder)
- Schubert Lieder, performed by Fischer-Dieskau/Moore, DG 437 214-2
- The Hyperion Schubert Edition, performed by Graham Johnson et al., 36 CD Series

Schubert, Franz. *Erlkönig*
- Fischer-Dieskau/Moore, DG 431 085 2, DG 453 676 2
- Goerne/Haefliger, Decca 4529172
- Terfel/Martineau, DG 445294 32
- Bostridge/Blake, EMI CDC 556347

Schubert, Franz. *Gretchen am Spinnrade*

- Popp/Johnson, Hyperion CDJ 33017
- Upshaw/Goode, Nonesuch 7559 79317-2
- Ameling/Baldwin, PHILIPS 420 870-2
- Janowicz/Gage, DG 453 082-2
- Auger/Orkis, Virgin 5614572
- Te Kanawa/Amner, Sony MK 39208

Schubert, Franz. *Die Forelle*

- Bär/Parsons, EMI CDC 754773 2
- Fleming/Eschenbach, Decca 455 294-2
- Mathis/Johnson, Hyperion CDJ 33021
- Wunderlich/Giesen, DG 447 452

Chopin, Frédéric. *Polonaise*, op. 53

- Alexander Brailowsky, Sony SBK 46546
- Artur Rubinstein, RCA 5615 2
- Vladimir Horowitz, CBS MK 42306
- Maurizio Pollini, EMI CDM7 69904 2
- Josef Lhévinne, Philips 456889 2
- Martha Argerich, EMI 7243 5 56805 2 5

Chopin, Frédéric. *Nocturnes*

- Artur Rubinstein, RCA Red Seal 5613-2, RCA D 89563
- Evgeny Kissin, RCA Victor 09026 60445 2
- Byron Janis, EMI Classics 56196
- Nelson Freire, Teldec 8.44076

Berlioz, Hector. *Symphonie fantastique*

- L'Orchestre Symphonique de Montréal, conducted by Charles Dutoit, Decca 458011
- Royal Concertgebouw of Amsterdam, conducted by Sir Colin Davies, Philips 464692
- The Cleveland Orchestra and Chorus, conducted by Pierre Boulez, DG 45343-2
- Chicago Symphony Orchestra, conducted by Daniel Barenboim, Teldec 4509-98800-2

Bizet, Georges. *Carmen*

- Price/Corelli/Freni/Merrill, Vienna State Opera Chorus, Vienna Philharmonic Orchestra, conducted by Herbert von Karajan, RCA 74321 39495-2
- Berganza/Domingo/Cotrubas/Milnes, Ambrosian Singers, London Symphony Orchestra, conducted by Claudio Abbado, DB 419 636-2
- Gheorgiu/Larmore/Moser/Ramey, Orchestra and Chorus of the Munich Staatsoper, conducted by Giuseppe Sinopoli, Teldec 0630 12672 2
- Ricciarelli/Baltsa/Carreras/Van Dam, Choir de l'Opera Paris, Berlin Philharmonic, conducted by Herbert von Karajan, DG 410 088-2
- Migenes-Johnson/Domingo/Raimondi/Esham, Orchestre National de France, conducted by Lorin Maazel, Erato 452072

Puccini, Giacomo. *Madama Butterfly*

- Freni/Pavarotti/Ludwig/Kerns, Vienna Philharmonic Orchestra, conducted by Herbert von Karajan, London 417 577-2
- Tebaldi/Bergonzi/Sordello/Cossotto, Santa Cecilia Academy Chorus and Orchestra, conducted by Tullio Serafin, Decca 425 531-2
- Scotto/di Stasio/Bergonzi/Panerai, Opera and Chorus of the Rome Opera, conducted by John Barbirolli, EMI CMS 7 69654 2

Debussy, Claude. *Prélude à l'après-midi d'un faune*

- The Cleveland Orchestra, conducted by Pierre Boulez, DG 435 766-2
- Montreal Symphony, conducted by Charles Dutoit, London 430240-2
- Philadelphia Orchestra, conducted by Eugene Ormandy, Sony SBK 53256
- Philharmonia Orchestra, conducted by Serge Baudo, CD-EMX 9502
- L'Orchestre de la Suisse Romande, conducted by Ernst Ansermet, DECCA 433 711-2
- Los Angeles Philharmonic, conducted by Esa-Pekka Salonen, Sony SK 62599

Stravinsky, Igor. *Petrushka*

- Boston Symphony Orchestra, conducted by Pierre Monteux, RCA 6529-2
- City of Birmingham Symphony Orchestra, conducted by Simon Rattle, EMI CDC 7 49503 2
- London Symphony Orchestra, conducted by Kent Nagano, Erato 3984-23142-2
- Royal Concertgebouw Orchestra, conducted by Sir Colin Davis, Philips 416 498-2
- Philadelphia Orchestra, conducted by Riccardo Muti, EMI CDC 7 47408 2
- The Cleveland Orchestra, conducted by Pierre Boulez, CBS MK 42395

Bernstein, Leonard. *West Side Story*

- Original Cast, Columbia SK 60724
- Los Angeles Philharmonic Orchestra, DG 410 025-2
- Symphonic Dances, Baltimore Symphony Orchestra, conducted by David Zinman London 452-916
- *The Songs of West Side Story*, RCA 62707

Louie, Alexina.

- *Music for Heaven and Earth*, Esprit Orchestra, conducted by Alex Pauk, CBC SMCD 5154
- *Canadian Music for Piano*, Louise Bessette, CBC MVCD 1064
- *Virtuoso Piano Music of Our Own Time*, Christina Petrowska, JLH 1002

APPENDIX C – LISTENING REPORT

We recommend that students listen to additional works besides those studied in detail. Teachers may wish to use this listening report template to make weekly listening assignments from the recommended listening lists provided for each composer studied.

Title ________________________________

Composer ________________________________

Genre ________________________________

Approximate date of composition ________________________________

Recording or Performance:

  Artist ________________________________

  Label ________________________________

Performing Forces ________________________________

Construction/Number of movements ________________________________

Summarize your impressions of this recording or performance by writing a brief review.